Listen To The Sphinx

A monumental work of the unknown, the spiritual, the alien, the occult, the future and the past.

See the world like never before, through the eyes of an Ipsissimus, both a Magi and an experimental technologist: A person who has worked with, and against, some of the most secretive groups and organizations on earth.

Stephen Templar reveals his work for the first time, exposing global conspiracies, lost secrets and the unknown.

Delve in to the depths of the multi-verse and discover the spiritual truth... that even the Aliens know.

Discover solutions for impossible problems and answers to some of the most important and perplexing questions ever asked.

From Lemurian computers and metaphysical technology to the limitless energy that powers them, from the Alien to the Divine, explore our universe and the unexpected truth in Listen To The Sphinx.

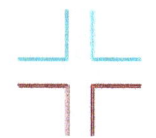

Listen To

The Sphinx

An Ipsissimus Breaks The Silence

By Rev. Dr. Stephen W. Templar, HKTB

Ivory Lady Publishing
Rescue, California

Copyright

Copyright © Stephen Templar, 2018

Published in the United States of America by
Ivory Lady Publishing; Rescue, California

All rights reserved.

Printed in the United States of America

No part of this publication may be reproduced or transmitted in any form or by any means, mechanical or electronic, including photocopying or recording, or by any information storage and retrieval system, or transmitted by email without permission in writing from the author. Reviewers may quote brief passages in reviews.

Neither the author nor the publisher assumes any responsibility for errors, omissions, or contrary interpretations of the subject matter herein. Any perceived slight of any individual or organization is purely unintentional.

Brand and product names are trademarks or registered trademarks of their respective owners.

Second Paperback Edition, 2018

ISBN: 978-0692197394

Cover Design by Ivory Lady Publishing

Dedication

For Morgan

Forever My Love

and

For Those

Who Are Ready

And Willing

Selected Contents

Title Page i
   Introduction iii
Begin.. 1
   The Flood!... 2
   Truth and Beauty 14
   Conversation with lcf.................................. 22
   Black & Wight... 24
   New Magical Numerology 36
   The New Era dawned 40
   Sacred Blade Oils...................................... 54
   Truth of Vril (Vrille) 56
   "Poem" 62
   Curses.. 68
   Lemurian (Symbol) Machine 70
   World Seed 76
   A Simple Elixir 86
   Color Plates.. 89
      Plate 1 89
      Plate 2 91
      Plate 3 93
      Plate 4 95
      Plate 5 97
      Plate 6 99
      Plate 7 101
      Plate 8 103
      Plate 9 105
      Plate 10 107
      Plate 11 109
   Healing Device... 112
   E's Den 120
   The End & The Beginning 122
   The Ark... 124
   Nephilim 130

Crystallization, Zyisian 138
On Demons, Devils, and Evil Beings 140
Solomon 142
Light Mites and Fallites 148
The Scroll of A'gypt 154
The End of Us 156
Anubis, Yin, Yang, Witches, Tengu 160
Magic and reality are the same. 168
Cthulhu / Cthulha / Cthulhin 176
What is Nirvana … 184
For some, they are not horns: 190
Color Plates 197
    Plate 12 197
    Plate 13 199
    Plate 14 201
    Plate 15 203
    Plate 16 205
    Plate 17 207
    Plate 18 209
    Plate 19 211
    Plate 20 213
Creation of Time 220
This War 228
Our Journey 230
Time Line of US 234
Endings 238
Children 240
Dragons 244
Listen to the Sphinx 248

…End 250

Appendix: A Templar's Thoughts 251

Color Plates Index

Plate 1: Clavicula Salomonis - Daniel Shulz
Plate 2: Le Veritable Dragon Rouge - Eric Santucci
Plate 3: King's Cup, Sumer - Stephen Templar
Plate 4: Peak Beyond The Wall - Stephen Templar
Plate 5: Ada and Eve - Stephen Templar
Plate 6: Spear and Knife - Stephen Templar
Plate 7: Always Watching - Stephen Templar
Plate 8: Sunrise, Black Forest, Germany - Bruno Wondrak
Plate 9: Red Stone - Stephen Templar
Plate 10: Saphiric Energy - Stephen Templar
Plate 11: A Special Mass - Erin Elizabeth
Plate 12: Sekhmet and Ptah - A. O. Darwish
Plate 13: Nefertiti - Stephen Templar
Plate 14: Tutankhaten - Stephen Templar
Plate 15: Wishing Cup - Stephen Templar
Plate 16: Princess Nsikhonsu's Ring - Stephen Templar
Plate 17: Sphinx Box, exterior - A. O. Darwish
Plate 18: Sphinx Box, interior - A. O. Darwish
Plate 19: Anubis - Stephen Templar
Plate 20: Ma'at - Stephen Templar

Listen To The Sphinx

An Ipsissimus Breaks The Silence

Introduction

There is a difference between that which is Secret and that which is Unknown. Many times, the unknown may be something that has yet to be discovered. At other times, the unknown may simply be that which has been lost... or even that which we refuse to accept.

We are all familiar with the concept of those things that were not true, until they were true: Beaked Whales, for example, even Giant Squid, the Northwest and Northeast Passages, Area 51, Ancient Greek Astrological & Astronomical Calculation Machines, Invisibility and that travel at The Speed of Sound is survivable and that travel faster than The Speed Of Light is possible.

While some of those things were bonafide secrets (State Secrets), others were not secrets at all and were known by those few people who had actually encountered them. We, in a general sense, considered some of those things to be unknown only because we refused to accept that those few who had actually encountered them were telling us the truth.

I have been blessed (and I use that work correctly) to have lived and known many Secrets. I have also had access to information that one can only describe as Unknown.

In my work in Law Enforcement I had the opportunity to rescue people from Satanic Cults and to study the Occult and to perform Exorcisms. Demonology, it seems, came naturally to me. For me, Ritual was no longer connected to Magic.

In my work in Experimental Technology I worked for a Private Government Contractor, on teams that developed and built systems for various entities and government agencies, including: DEA & NASA. I worked on technologies that have impacted all of our lives, yet many are still Secret or Unknown.

Later in my life those two worlds would collide. In that moment I found myself identifying and developing Metaphysical Technologies. Exploring the boundaries between the Known, the Secret and the Unknown became my specialty. Identifying which threats came from Us and which threats came from Others and which threats which threats came from sources that were Unknown to Us consumed a significant part of my life.

This time in my life was enlightening. Soon, the Unknown was rarely Unknowable and Secrets were no longer describable as such. As the walls collapsed and the barriers faded away, that is when the Veils ceased to exist and one lesson became paramount: Truth is absolute! It has no point of view.

In that time I kept journals, because many of the things that I was exploring could not be called Secrets, they were exclusively within the domain of the Unknown.

There are no rules or regulations governing the Unknown, except by those who only imagine that they have power. There is one exception to this concept, you will know it when you encounter it: It involves our relationship to a fellow called: Elohim (many call him God).

When he and his wife created this opportunity for Us, to grow beyond our eternal immortal selves, they did so by offering us the one thing that we could not know: Limitation.

They stepped out of the world from which we came, into what the Hebrews call the Middle World (A place that bridges the gap between that place which we are from and this place, where we presently are).

From this Middle World they created a new Limited (Read: Physical) World which forced those of us who volunteered into a Limited Physical Reality. A reality dominated by measures, such as distance and time, in which our eternal immortal selves could not exist without experiencing Cause and Effect, Interconnectedness, Loss and Death.

This Limited World provides us the opportunity to understand aspects of existence that were meaningless to Us where we are from. The eternal and immortal do not bleed, they do not feel pain, nor can they comprehend consequences. Empathy is beyond us there too, leaving little doubt as to why we needed an opportunity to grow.

Interestingly, the concepts of Secrets and the Unknown also do not exist where we are from. Which is why it is no great surprise that some of those who did not volunteer to come to this Limited World choose to invade it. We call them Demons or Devils and many more names from the many cultures on Earth.

While there are those Uninvited who push through, in truth there are only two who can violate the rules of this Limited World without the assistance of someone legitimately dwelling within it, we call them God, or Elohim and Ti (his wife).

What follows is a Journal. Hand written, by me, over a period of many years, this journal contains many events and descriptions of what I encountered that we can safely classify as Unknown.

For clarity, a typed transcript of the text on each page appears on the facing page. Symbols and sketches are not reproduced… only the original hand drawn content is provided.

These journal entries are not presented in any particular order. Two separate journals are presented and, therefore, the timeline from beginning to end is not linear.

Similarly, the events and subjects are presented as they happened. No attempt to reorganize this information, for clarity or otherwise, has been made.

Also, recognize that in some cases there may be multiple entries for what appear to be similar circumstances or events. These entries are presented as they occurred and, as a result, some observations were made after I gained additional experience or increased access. At other times, two things that appear to be contradictory are actually addressing two entirely different things, with similar names.

What I present here is for posterity, and for those who are ready, willing and able to accept it. There will be no debate about this information, not with me. What I present here is Truth. Accept it, or do not.

If you can accept what I have witnessed, then I promise you that you will see the world through new eyes, you will begin to understand things that others consider to be Unknown.

Begin…

The Flood!

70,000 years ago, The Flood was more than just a drop in the oceans of Earth. While it did manifest as water, thousands of feet of it, here on Earth; it also impacted the rest of created physical reality.

The divine experiment, to allow the eternal and omnipotent to experience limited linear being by possessing limited physical bodies, extended far beyond the Earth.

The Earthly attempts, such as Octopi and Saurians, did not work. They could not survive the presence of an eternal soul. Finally, on Earth, 1.283 million years ago, there was success … Humans could survive, and the rest is our history.

Other worlds and types of life were ready and able long before the people of Earth. In fact, the universe (multi-verse) was teaming with soul-bearing life forms.

For nearly two billion years, The Divine Souls inhabited various beings of the created physical universe, and many of its dimensions.

continued ->

The Flood!

70,000 years ago, The Flood was more than just a drop in the oceans of Earth. While it did manifest as water, thousands of feet of it, here on Earth; it also impacted the rest of created physical reality.

The divine experiment, to allow the eternal and omnipotent to experience limited linear being by possessing limited physical bodies, extended far beyond the Earth.

The Earthly attempts, such as Octopi and Saurians did not work. They could not survive the presence of an eternal soul. Finally, on Earth, 1.283 million years ago there was success... Humans could survive, and the rest is our history.

Other worlds and types of life were ready and able long before the people of Earth. In fact, the universe (multi-verse) was teaming with soul bearing life forms.

For nearly two billion years the Divine Souls inhabited various beings of the created physical universe, and many of its dimensions.

→

<-- continued from above

Then came the flood! In that moment, everyone was gone. Everyone except for one earthbound human male and his family.

For all intents and purposes, it was over … the reset button had been pushed, leaving just one family of true souls to begin again.

For the descendants of that family, those who come after us and who exist in a universe of interdimensional travel and time manipulation, the universe was suddenly empty. Like a rapture, it left them mystified. They were alone in the universe, able only to establish that everyone who was left were descended from one man, on one tiny water planet called Earth.

What's more, a short time after the Flood, even the souls of the Earth left the universe, never to be seen or detected again. This created a new question: What were these souls, where did they come from, and where did they go? Perhaps most importantly, they were now in a position to wonder what they, themselves were (are) … this is one of the most important questions ever asked!

continued ->

Then came the flood! In that moment everyone was gone. Everyone except for one earthbound human male and his family.

For all intents and purposes it was over... the reset button had been pushed, leaving just one family of true Souls to begin again.

For the decendants of that family, those who came after us and who exist in a universe of interdimensional travel and time manipulation, the universe was suddenly empty. Likee a rapture it left them mystified. They were alone in the universe, able only to establish that everyone who was left were decended from one man, on one tiny water planet called Earth.

What's more, a short time after the Flood, even the souls of the Earth left the universe, never to be seen or detected again. This created a new question: What were these souls, where did they come from, where did they go? Perhaps most importantly, they were now in a possitron to wonder what they, themselves, were (are)... This is one of the most important questions ever asked!

⟶

The descendants of US, thanks to their technological advantages, could remember that there had been souls everywhere in the universe. They could identify when the souls left the universe. They even knew that one small ocean planet, Earth, still had souls for over 70,000 years after the others vanished. A drop in the proverbial bucket, to be sure, but a very significant drop indeed.

The lesson in this is that this tiny infinite universe of infinite dimensions, but of limited Time, contains something called Spirit or Life Energy. This is entirely different from the mysterious souls of the Divine Possessors. Spirit is a fundamental layer, or aspect, of the physical reality. Spirit crosses dimensions in ways that other aspects of being may not. Spirit is the difference between alive and not alive, even though our current earthly ideas and perceptions on this subject are quite limited.

Spirit and the Soul are very different things. All living things contain Spirit, but comparatively few ever possessed (or were possessed by) a Soul.

The decendants of US, thanks to their technological advantages, could remember that there had been souls every where in the universe. They could identify when the souls left the universe. They even knew that one small ocean planet, Earth, still had souls for over 70,000 years after the others vanished. A drop in the proverbial bucket, to be sure, but a very significant drop indeed.

The lesson in this is that this tiny infinite universe of infinite dimensions, but of limited Time, contains something called Spirit or Life Energy. This is entirely different from the mysterious souls of the divine possessors. Spirit is a fundimental layer, or aspect, of the physical reality. Spirit crosses dimensions in ways that other aspects of being may not. Spirit is the difference between alive and not alive, even though our current earthly ideas and perceptions on this subject are quite limited.

Spirit and the Soul are very different things. All living things contain Spirit, but comparitively few ever possessed (or were possessed by) a Soul.

In the physical universe, every living thing contains Spirit. Spirit is that aspect of being that is life.

The Divine Soul comes from somewhere beyond the physical. They may possess a physical Spirit containing being.

When a physical Spirit containing being that is possessed by a Soul dies, the Soul moves on. Either returning to where it is originally from or transferring itself to another physical spirit containing being (something we call reincarnation).

Because Souls hail from beyond the measures of distance and time, the reincarnated may present themselves in any place, any dimension, in any time within the limitations of the infinite physical reality.

Spirit is every living thing in physical reality.

Souls, though detectible, are immeasurable and exist beyond the confines of the infinite physical reality, even when they are here.

In the physical universe, every living thing contains Spirit. Spirit is that aspect of being that is life.

The Divine Soul comes from somewhere beyond the physical. They may possess a physical Spirit containing being.

When a physical Spirit containing being that is possessed by a Soul dies, the Soul moves on. Either returning to where it is originally from or transferring itself to another physical Spirit containing being (something we call reincarnation).

Because Souls hail from beyond the measures of distance and time, the reincarnated may present themselves in any place, any dimension, in any time within the limitations of the infinite physical reality.

Spirit is every living thing in physical reality.

Souls, though detectible, are immeasurable and exist beyond the confines the infinite physical reality, even when they are here.

This journal contains the collected notes and observations, pertaining to life, religion, metaphysics and the occult of Dr. Stephen William Templar, known to some as *The Dragon King*.

-ST

If you are infinite and omnipotent, what excuse do you have not to live, not to do?!?!

-ST

What is written in this journal may not appear in chronological order. But, it is all true; it all happened…every word!

-ST

God created the universe and all of the Alien's know it. Because, they are aware that they all descended from us. Even those that seem to predate us actually are our descendants. They come here and study us because the one mystery they cannot solve is our souls. We have them, here and now, but they do not. They can detect, even fake, a soul, but they do not understand or have souls themselves.

This journal contains the collected notes and observations, pertaining to life, religion, metaphysics and the occult, of Dr. Stephen William Templar, known to some as The Dragon King.

If you are infinite and omnipotent, what excuse do you have not to live, not to do ?!?!

What is written in this journal may not appear in chronological order. But, it is all true; it all happened... every word!

God created the universe and all of the Alien's know it. Because, they are aware that they all decended from us. Even those that seem to predate us actually are our decendants. They come here and study us because the one mystery they cannot solve is our souls. We have them here and now, but they do not. They can detect, even fake, a soul, but they do not understand or have souls themselves.

Perception is key, what might be usable light to one person will be unusable light to another. This "perception" aspect of the observable universe is why some people see something, where others do not, even when they are all observing the same thing.

Perfect cop partners or sniper/spotter partners might be amazing together. Either because their perceptions are so similar or because they are complimentary.

Split these partners up to create two other teams, each with one of them, and you may not ever get similar outstanding performance from either of the new teams.

Incompatible or non-complimentary perceptions may impact every sort of relationship, from co-workers to married couples. Frequently, perfect unions are a result of compatible perceptions.

In one of you sees a space craft and the other sees a bird, hope to God that you are looking at different Things. If not, then at least one of you is in trouble.

continued ->

Perception is key, what might be usable light to one person will be unusable light to another. This "perception" aspect of the observable universe is why some people see something, where others do not, even when they are all observing the same thing.

Perfect cop partners or sniper/spotter partners might be amazing together, either because their perceptions are so similar or because they are complimentary.

Split those partners up to create two other teams, each with one of them, and you may not ever get similar outstanding performance from either of the new teams.

Incompatible or non-complimentary perceptions may impact every sort of relationship, from co-workers to married couples. Frequently, perfect unions are a result of compatible perceptions.

If one of you sees a space craft and the other sees a bird, hope to God that you are looking at different things. If not, then at least one of you is in trouble.

→

Perception also applies to non-visible aspects of the universe: Good vs. Evil being on area most notably impacted by perception.

Do not confuse perception with Interpretation or Choices.

Truth and Beauty

Consider the great serpent god of the Aztecs:

To them, He was a divine serpent-man that flew down, personally from the heavens, to interact with them by some sort of divine magic.

Many 21st century interpretations of that God use the idea of, "Any technology significantly beyond your own will appear to be magic," as a way to claim that the Aztec people had been visited by Alien beings.

As usual, the actual truth falls in between, what seems to be a reasonably thought-out truth to describe the absolutely beautiful story, as interpreted by the ancients.

continued ->

Perception also applies to non-visible aspects of the universe: Good vs Evil being one area most notably impacted by perception.

Do not confuse Perception with Interpretation or Choices.

Truth + Beauty

Consider the great serpent god of the Aztecs:

To them, he was a divine serpentman that flew down, presumably from the heavens, to interact with them by some sort of divine magic.

Many 21st century interpretations of that god use the idea of, "any technology significantly beyond your own will appear to be magic", as a way to claim that the Aztec people had been visited by Alien beings.

As usual, the actual truth falls in between, what seems to be a reasonably thought out truth to describe the absolutely beautiful story, as interpreted by the ancients.

⟶

In fact, neither "The Truth" nor "The Beautiful" is accurate, in terms of physical reality.

The individual in question is neither the God of The Beautiful Aztec story, nor the described "Alien" from another world that so many have accepted as The Truth.

In reality, this being was a man that happened to have the appearance of a serpent, as the result of the same divine curse that left him trapped on Earth for long as We (the proverbial We) have been here.

His ability to "fly" was actually based on technology, but it was not "alien" technology. This man's "hand" can be seen in many of the great cultures throughout history, as can his depicted image.

While this man often offered to help leaders/rulers to achieve their goals or to obtain their desires, his intent was always selfish: What you got was only important to you because you perceived it as such. This man could easily allow anyone to have what they desired because he, himself, knew what really mattered, what was truly valuable and important.
continued ->

In fact, neither "The Truth" nor "The Beautiful" is accurate, in terms of physical reality.

The individual in question is neither the god of the beautiful Aztec story, nor the described "Alien" from another world that so many have accepted as the truth.

In reality, this being was a man that happened to have the appearance of a serpent, as a result of the same divine curse that left him trapped on Earth for as we (the Proverbial we) have been here.

His ability to "fly" was actually based on technology, but it was not "alien" technology. This man's "hand" can be seen in many of the great cultures throughout history, as can his depicted image.

While this man often offered to help leaders/rulers to achieve their goals or to obtain their desires, his intent was always selfish: what you get was only important to you because you perceived it as such. This man could easily allow anyone to have what they desired because he, himself, knew what really mattered, what was truly valuable and important. ⟶

Or, so he thought! In the end he discovered that he had deceived even himself. Only at the end did this "divine snake god"/"Alien" learn the value of what dwells in both truth and beauty. Only in death did this "immortal" understand that he had been a pawn in his own game. And, that immortality, like power, can be a gift or a curse, and sometimes it is just life.

To be or not to be is not really the question. To do or not to, that is a question that we can actually work with. As for being, if you are, then you always have been, and you always will be. If you are not, then the matter is moot.

If you are, and you only exist in the physical universe ("Creation") then, chances are, you are wearing a watch and the concept of immortality is not relevant for you. Work on it, if you wish. But, don't be disappointed if it eludes you.
Time, space, existence, beginning and end; these things are very real, and they genuinely matter…to some people.

Or, so he thought! In the end he discovered that he had deceived even himself. Only at the end did this "divine snake god"/"Amen" learn the value of what dwells in both truth and beauty. Only in death did this "imortal" understand that he had been a pawn in his own game. And, that imortality, like power, can be a gift or a curse, and sometimes it is just life.

— — — — — — — —

To be or not to be is not really the question. ~~To be~~ To do or not to, that is a question that we can actually work with. As for being, if you are, then you always have been and you always will be.
If you are not, then the matter is moot.
If you are, and you only exist in the physical universe ("creation") then, chances are, you are wearing a watch and the concept of imortality is not relevent for you. Work on it, if you wish. But, don't be disapointed if it elludes you.
Time, space, existance, beginning and end; these things are very real and they genuinely matter... to some people.

Metatechnology comes with new problems: there are meta-beings that live in realities that overlap our metaphysical…to them, our metaphysical is their physical.

Sometimes, when matter seems to vanish from our reality, it is just that someone/thing ate it or used it in a different reality.

Time can be edited. Some spend considerable resources trying to edit time to achieve a future in which more than 5$ of humans might survive the Ice Age (Glacial State).

We all make mistakes: human footprints fossilized next to dinosaur tracks, Thor's Hammer, Atlantis…Sometimes our future becomes our past.

Metatechnology comes with new problems: There are metabeings that live in realities that overlap our metaphysical... to them, our metaphysical is their physical.

Sometimes, when matter seems to vanish from our reality, it is just that someone/thing ate it or used it in a different reality.

Time can be edited. Some spend considerable resources trying to edit time to achieve a future in which more than 5% of humans might survive the next Ice Age.

We all make mistakes: human footprints fossilized next to dinosaur tracks, Thor's Hammer, Atlantis... Sometimes our future becomes our past.

20 Jan 2017

Conversation with lcf...

lcf: ST, I knew there was darkness within you.

I did not know; that darkness is what the Russian's seek.

The well of souls.

The Heart of Darkness.

A dragon's Heart. I did not know.

And then: his Faustian moment came; His first; because he was unbroken.

                                                                        -ST

— — — — — — — — — — — — — — — —

The Unicorn horn destroys negative energy creatures.

20 Jan 2017
    Conversation with lcf...

  lcf: $, I knew there was darkness within you.

        I did not know; that darkness is what
        the Russians seek.

        The well of souls.

        The Heart of Darkness.

        A Dragon's Heart. I did not know.

   and then: his Faustian Moment came; His first,
   because he was unbroken.
                                        $

   — — — — —   —   —

The Unicorn horn destroys negative energy creatures.

4 Sept 2017

3.5 trillion years of back and forth, of evolution and advancement…the result was a being that was not worth living.

Time stopped when the Dragon ate creation.

The universe, creation, did not cease when time was removed…but who could tell…and, how could they?!?!

———————————————

5 Sept 2017

Black & Wight

The Black Knife is a blade that burns within. The inner fire is the Black Fire of Lucifer. It burns!
Access to the Black Fire is obtained only after the Faustian Moment. In a sense, you must fail to achieve it…so, don't be too proud.

The Wight Knife is a blade that contains the light (lifeforce) of The Great Wight. A man-like creature that consumed men in an attempt to gain their power…their souls.

It succeeded in absorbing six souls. Each like a multiple personality, but without the linear time split. All six at once, all the time.

continued ->

4 Sept. 2017

    3.5 trillion years of back and forth, of evolution and advancement... the result was a being that was not worth living.

    Time stopped when the Dragon ate creation.

    The universe, creation, did not cease when time was removed... but, who could tell... and, how could they ?!?!

— —

5 Sept. 2017

Black + Wight

The Black Knife is a blade that burns within. The inner fire is the Black Fire, of Lucifer. It burns! Access to the Black Fire is obtained only after the Faustian Moment. In a sense, you must fail to achieve it... so, don't be too proud.

The Wight Knife is a blade that contains the light (life force) of the Great Wight. A man like creature that consumed men in an attempt to gain their power... their souls.

It succeeded in absorbing six souls. Each like a multiple personality, but without the linear time split. All six at once, all the time. →

In time the Wight began seeking and consuming the possessed, in an attempt to find something that could overcome the chaos of the multiple souls. It did find it. A demon, the most powerful demonic energy ever to exist in creation. The demon was Sephistophole. It trapped the Wight in crystalline steel. This was the origin of the story and reality of the Wight Knife. A true Wight Knife contains the energy of the eternal Wight and the binding demonic life energy of Sephistophole.

There have ever been only 8 Wight Knives.

In time the Wight began seeking and consuming the possessed, in an attempt to find something that could overcome the chaos of the multiple souls. It did find it. A demon, the most powerful demonic energy ever to exist in creation. The demon was Sephistophele. It trapped the Wight in crystaline steel. This was the original the story and reality of the Wight Knife. A true Wight Knife contains the energy of the actual Wight and the binding demonic life energy of Sephistophele.
There have ever been only 8 Wight Knives.

16 Sept. 2017

Jack died today. He's a good man, and he is home now…w/Elohim (Yeshua doesn't play golf).

I was reminded today: Regarding Death's

To us, here in creation, Deaths seem imposing, even terrifying. Harbingers of change; a scary sort of change.

To the proverbial Us, spiritual or heavenly or metaphysical (as you wish), the opportunity to serve as a Death is a great thing, a high honor…to be an Angel, but more than that, to be an Angel who is tasked with helping and guiding us, not to an after-life, but rather: To Our Home.
    The job of "Death" is to guide us home. What greater opportunity could an Angel hope for than to get to bring us home.

To be a Death is a joyous and magnificent opportunity. To meet one, well, that is how we return home. Celebrate!

16 Sept. 2017

Jack died today. He's a good man, and he is home now... w/ Elohim (Yeshua doesn't play golf).

I was reminded today: Regarding Deaths

To us, here in creation, Deaths seem imposing, even terrifying. Harbingers of change; a scary sort of change.

To the proverbial us, spiritual or heavenly or meta-physical (as you wish) the opportunity to serve as a Death is a great thing, a high honor... to be an Angel, but more than that, to be an Angel ~~xxxxx~~ who is tasked with helping and guiding us, not to an after-life, but rather: To Our Home.
The job of Death is to guide us home. What greater opportunity could an Angel hope for than to get to bring us home.
To be a Death is a joyous and magnificent opportunity. To meet one, well, that is how we return home. Celebrate!

To the infinite, anything less than infinite was nothing.

That is the lesson of this place, creation.

Nothing that is, is less than infinite.

Said again:

Nothing that is, is less than infinite.

— — —

When we leave this place, we will close the door behind us. That does not mean that this place is nothing.

— — —

The scroll of creation: (symbol)
The fire of creation: (symbol)

The serpent of creation: (symbol)
The binding of creation: (symbol)

To the infinite, anything less than infinite was nothing.

That is the lesson of this place, creation.

Nothing that is, is less than infinite.

Said again:

Nothing that is, is less than infinite.

When we leave this place, we will close the door behind us.
That does not mean that this place is nothing.

The scroll of creation: 📝
The fire of creation: 🔥

The serpent of creation ∽
The binding of creation ○

21 Sept. 2017

We who dwelt On High, were the chosen.
Those who dwelt below, were the snakes of the earth.
As the year ends, we are no longer divided.
As the new year begins, we all belong to God.

- MT & ST

- Thus endeth the year 5777
Thus begineth the year 5778 –

(Symbol)

Less than everything, is not nothing
Less than perfection, is not nothing
- This is the nature of forgiveness.

- ST

21 Sept 2017

We who dwelt on high, were the chosen.
Those who dwelt below, were the snakes
    of the earth.
As the year ends, we are no longer divided.
As the new year begins, we all belong to God.

$

— Thus endeth the year 5777
  Thus begineth the year 5778 —

Less than everything, is not nothing.
Less than perfection, is not nothing.
— This is the nature of forgiveness.

$

When pondering the word of God, there is this:

What is written and what was spoken are not the same.

What was spoken, that is truth.

What is written, that is to inspire others to seek the truth.

———————————————————

Traditional reincarnation is not correct!
My idea of multiple coexistence is closer, but still not it.

———————————————————

3 people have successfully hunted Tyrannosaurus Rex. No single person has ever killed more than 5 (6) T. Rex. In that case they had killed 5 in hunts. They were after #6 when it accidentally killed itself. Humans have killed more than 2,500 T. Rex.
Isn't "Time" interesting?!

When pondering the word of God, there is this:

What is written and what was spoken are not the same.

What was spoken, that is truth.

What is written, that is to inspire others to seek the truth.

— — — — — — —

Traditional reincarnation is not correct!
My idea of multiple coexistance is closer, but still not it.

— — — — — — —

3 people have successfully hunted T. rex. No single person has ever killed more than 5 (6) T. rex. In that case they had killed 5 in hunts, they were after #6 when it accidentally killed itself. Humans have killed more than 2,500 T. rex. Isn't "time" interesting!

6 Jan. 2018

New Magical Numerology: Things Changed!

A	7		X	7
B	1		Y	5
C	4		Z	1
D	3			
E	2			
F	5			
G	8			
H	9			
I	5/50 (final)			
J	50			
K	11			
L	3			
M	14			
N	72			
O	12			
P	3			
Q	4			
R	6			
S	3			
T	2			
U	5			
V	6			
W	8			

6 Jan. 2008

New Magical Numerology : Things Changed!

A	7	X	7
B	1	Y	5
C	4	Z	1
D	3		
E	2		
F	5		
G	8		
H	9		
i	5/50 (final)		
J	50		
K	11		
L	3		
M	14		
N	72		
O	12		
P	3		
Q	4		
R	6		
S	3		
T	2		
U	5		
V	6		
W	8		

(Symbol) *Days On Earth*

"*Redacted*" days

- Or -

"*Redacted*" years

200"*Redacted*" years

The last of "us" will leave in "*Redacted*"

The first "*Redacted*" will be announced in 2168

The last of "us" "*Redacted*" in "*Redacted*" ~ about 11:38 am MT (18:38 GMT)"

The first "non-us" "*Redacted*" in the same minute.

△ Days On Earth

"Redacted" days

—or—

"Redacted" yrs.

2α "Redacted" yrs.

The last of "us" will leave in "Redacted"

The first "Redacted" will be announced in 2/68

The last of "us" "Redacted" n "Redacted" @ 11:38 am MT (18:38 GMT)

The first "non-us" "Redacted" in the same minute.

30 March 2010 about 12:21:30 Eastern Time

The New Era dawned. The old world ended and the new one began. The eternal brilliance of humanity has begun, in earnest.

L+L+C have signed their names in The Book and sworn their eternal allegiance to The One and his goals: Their continued existence and involvement at his will alone.

The entire event was witnessed by: EAJ (I)

(Symbol)   - ST

30 March 2010 @ 12:21:30 Eastern Time

 The New Era dawned. The old world ended and the new one began. The eternal brilliance of humanity has begun, in ernest.

 L+L+C have signed their names in the book and sworn their eternal allegiance to The One and his goals: Their continued existance and involvement at his will alone.

The entire event was witnessed by: EAJ(I)

△ $

Atlantis – Tengu – Ravens

Late 2022 – Early 2023

A Time experiment sends a US nuclear aircraft carrier back to pre-Greece: That carrier becomes Atlantis. The plan is that they will go unnoticed and, if seen, they will be written off to history as Crete (benefit of hind-sight).

They become trapped due to equipment failure.
C/Kain discovers their presence and, eventually, musters an attack. C/Kain loses thousands of soldiers in the attack, but he succeeds in destroying the carrier.

Two groups use what limited Time-tech they have and can assemble to flee, in an attempt to get home.

Long story short: One group becomes the Tengu, in Japan. The other group becomes the Norse Gods of Vikingdom.

The Norse Gods go completely unnoticed by C/Kain. The Tengu are, eventually, discovered and realize that their only hope is to flee to a time before the

continued ->

Atlantis — Tengu — Ravens
Late 2022 — Early 2023

A Time experiment sends a US nuclear aircraft carrier back to pre-Greece: That carrier becomes Atlantis. The plan is that they will go unnoticed and, if seen, they will be written off to history as Crete. (benefit of hind-sight)

They become trapped due to equipment failure. C/Kain discovers their presence and, eventually, musters an attack. C/Kane loses thousands of soldiers in the attack, but he succeeds in destroying the carrier.

Two groups use what limited time/tech they have and can assemble to flee, in an attempt to get home.

Long story short: One group becomes the Tengu, in Japan. The other group becomes the Norse Gods of Vikingdom.

The Norse Gods go completely unnoticed by C/Kain. ~~because~~ They now pre-exist any event of which C/Kane is ~~aware~~. The Tengu are, eventually, discovered and realize that their only hope is to flee to a time before the

⟶

<-- continued from above

original conflict with C/Kain, so he will have no memory of them yet.

They vanish into the past and help the pre-Viking culture become the builders/suppliers of the Bronze Age. They do this as "The Ravens" – the Tengu concept works again, this time as The Ravens. This is safe because they know what "gods" are coming. The Ravens build toward that eventual society.

Those who escape to become the Norse Gods step into roles that pre-date them. This is ultimately how they go unnoticed by C/Kain.

None of the crew of the "Atlantis" ever make it home to the 21st century.

(Symbol)   -ST

The Boat:
- Thor: CQC w/pair of Sig Sauer 1911's
- Freya: Pilot – likes M4, but uses Rem .700 in .308 when needed
- Odin: Tech guy – works TDE
- Sniper: Splinched during first jump

continued ->

←

Original conflict with C/Kane, so he will have no memory of them yet.
They vanish into the past and help the pre-Viking culture become the builders/suppliers of the Bronze Age. They do this as "The Ravens" - the Tengu concept works again, this time as The Ravens. This is safe because they know what "gods" are coming. The Ravens build toward that, eventual, society.

Those who escape to become the Norse Gods step into roles that pre-date them, this is ultimately how they go unnoticed, by C/Kain.

None of the crew of the "Atlantis" ever make it home, to the 21st century.

△ $

The Boat:
Thor: CQC w/ pair Sig Sauer 1911's
Freya: Pilot - likes M4, but used Rem. 700 in 308 when needed.
Odin: Tech. guy - works TDE
Sniper: Splinched during first jump.

→

<-- continued from above

    Medic: Became Caine (after unexpected successful hunt)

    "Other Guy": Made poor choices – all that is said!

Medic: Thought that if they killed C/Kain with drugs then no one would have to pay…he was wrong!

Odin: Time Displacement Equipment expert – there had been a British soldier on the Big Ship, but when he died…and Odin volunteered for the "rescue mission," they gave Odin the Brit's SA80 with bayonet and CQB sight. That came to be known as "Odin's Spear"!

Freya: could shoot – if Thor or Odin needed to do something impressive. Then she would conceal herself and use the Rem .308 to make the "impossible shot." The rifle had an Audio Baffle, so only the sonic booms were generally audible.

Thor: was Mexican/Irish and was tough and hard. He was a CQC specialist: knives, axes, 1911's, hands, feet etc. He was a CQC badass!

← Medic: became Caine (after unexpected successful hunt)
"Other Guy": made poor choices — all that is sand!

Medic: Thought that if they killed Caine with drugs then no one would have to pay... he was wrong!

Odin: Time Displacement Equipment expert — there had been a British soldier on the Big Ship, but when he died... and Odin volunteered for "rescue mission" — They gave Odin the Brit's SA80 w/ bayonet and CQB sight. That came to be known as Odin's Spear!

Freya: could shoot — if Thor or Odin needed to do something impressive, then she would conceal herself and use the Rem. 308 to make the "impossible shot". The rifle had an Audio Baffle, so only the sonic booms were generally audible.

Thor: was Mexican/Irish and was tough and hard. He was a CQC specialist: knives, axes, 1911's, hands, feet, etc. — he was a CQC badass!

EMP

Directed EMP is a reality! It takes the full sphere of EMP and redirects it to a focused direction 8° to 18° min/max: 12° options for weapon use.

Conversation with Thor, Michael E., Odin & Freya:

Fewer and Shorter "wires" (traces) makes sight, etc., more likely to survive an EMP.

For Sights: Choose Dials or Switches over Buttons.

Heavy and Thick metals over light plastics.

AimPoint does well, but Eotech does not!
    50% of Eotechs fail!
    80% of AimPoints survive! (with buttons = 50 – 60%)

Chinese and Korean stuff fails: Almost Universally!

Pre-2012 Russian stuff fairs pretty well!

USA, Japan, Israel, High-End European: All Good!
High quality beats Low quality almost always - all else being equal

                                              continued ->

EMP

Directed EMP is a reality! It takes the full sphere of EMP and redirects it to a focused direction 8° – 18° min/max : 12° optimal for weapon use.

Conversation w/ Thor, Michael E., Odin + Freya :

Fewer and Shorter "wires" (traces) makes sights, etc., more likely to survive an EMP.

For Sights : choose Dials or ~~Keys~~ switches over buttons.

Heavy + Thick metals over light plastics.

AimPoint does well, but Eotech does not!
    50% of Eotechs fail!
    80% of ~~Aim~~Points survive! (w/buttons = 50-60%)

Chinese + Korean stuff fails : Almost Universally!

Pre 2012 Russian stuff fairs pretty well!

USA, Japan, Israel, High End European : All Good!

High quality beats low quality almost ~~universally~~ all else being equal →

<-- continued from above

Clean finishes help – cerekote, parkerization, etc.

Being mounted on a weapon that is not touching metal is almost as good as a Faraday Cage.

Highest rate of EMP survival is AimPoint Comp M4 (85 – 90%)

Compact Bushnell and similar with knobs are good (65%)

UltraDot with knobs are good (70-75%)

"Glass scopes don't fail, until they break!"

More notes:

If that day comes SWT/MAT cannot head to Kansas. Too many things will follow you there. They have a better chance without you and your baggage.

When setting up EMP boxes, be sure each one has a weapon immediately ready inside.

When setting up lenses, be sure to conceal weapons and armor from plain sight. Secrecy is important and…

continued ->

←

clean finishes help — cerekote, parkerization, etc.

Being mounted on a weapon that is not touching metal is almost as good as a Faraday Cage.

Highest rate of EMP survival is AimPoint Comp M4 (85-90%)

Compact Bushnell and Similar w/ knobs are good (65%)

UltraDot w/ knobs are good (70-75%)

"Glass scopes don't fail, until they break!"

More Notes:
   If that day comes SWT/MAT cannot head to Kansas. Too many things will follow you there. They have a better chance without you, and your baggage.

When setting up EMP boxes, be sure each one has a weapon immediately ready inside.

When setting up houses be sure to conceal weapons and Armor from plain sight. Secrecy is important and...
→

<-- continued from above

...necessary. Friends should know, but others should not.

Be prepared: some low level, brittle polymers are actually weakened by EMP and similar fields.

Just be aware, prepared, and careful!

From Thor: Don't every sell/trade any of The Three Giant Swords, except to Close Friends. Nothing that may be gained is worth more!

Any EMP "attack" that is not a direct nuclear attack/strike is "Fake!"

Truth: The Nuke has a greater terminal radius than the EMP does.

There are plans to "Fake" EMP attacks to create regional and localized setbacks as well as to prompt conflict(s).

... necessary. Friends should know, but others should not.

Be prepared: some low level, brittle, polymers are actually weakened by EMP and similar fields. Just be aware, prepared and careful!

From Thor: Do not ever sell/trade any of the Three Giant Swords, except to close friends. Nothing, that might be gained, is worth more!

Any EMP "attack" that is not a direct nuclear attack/strike is "Fake"! Truth: The Nuke has a greater terminal radius than the EMP does.

There are plans to "Fake" EMP attacks to create regional and localized set backs as well as to prompt conflict(s).

Sacred Blade Oils

- Tsubaki-Abura (Camellia Oil)
- Calamus Oil (Daemomorops Draco – Calamus Draco)
- Hinoki Oil (sacred trees – only in Japan and Oregon)
- Choji Oil (Clove Oil)

Traditional Choji Oil for Katana:
- 80 parts – Camellia
- 4 parts – Choji
- 1 part – Calamus

Sacred Oil for Katana:
- 80 parts – Camellia
- 4 parts – Hinoki
- 1 part – Calamus

Sacred Blade Oils
- Tsubaki-Abura (Camellia Oil)
- Calamus Oil (Daemonorops Draco - Calamus Draco)
- Hinoki Oil (sacred trees - only in Japan + Oregon)
- Choji Oil (clove Oil)

Traditional Choji Oil for Katana:
- 80 parts - Camellia
- 4 parts - Choji
- 1 part - Calamus

Sacred Oil for Katana:
- 80 parts - Camellia
- 4 parts - Hinoki
- 1 part - Calamus

Truth of Vril (Vrille)

A group from "our" point of origin, fearing that the dangerous Elohim might use the experience(s) to take sole control of "everything," forced an oversight group into the experiment. They live in the true physical, but without the true limits of survival (much like the proverbial Octopus). Without limitations or fear, they do what they can to stand in the way of anything that they suspect might enable Elohim to rise and grow. They care nothing for the experience, but often support any enemy of Elohim, simply out of spite.

An early, massively successful, experiment was highjacked by these overseers and the people that they took over "for study and examination" were enslaved and forced ("freed") to build a "home" for the overseers. This home can be described as a single "flying disc" that measures 26,700 miles in circumference. The ship is (was) powered by a Devil (not a demon, but the parent of demons) called Sheen…

With no lifespan and a home with an unlimited power supply, these overseers extended themselves fully into the physical, where they destroy/hinder any (one/thing/etc.) that the think might empower Elohim further. They have been known to park their home/ship between a planet and

continued ->

Truth of Vril (Vrille)

A group from "our" point of origin, fearing that the dangerous Elohim might use the experience(s) to take sole control of "everything", forced an oversight group into the experiment. They live in the true physical, but without the true limits of survival (much like the proverbial Octopus). Without limitations or fear, they do what they can to stand in the way of anything that they suspect might enable Elohim to rise and grow. They care nothing for the experience, but often support any enemy of Elohim, simply out of spite. An early, massively successful, experiment was highjacked by these overseers and the people that they took over "for study and examination" were enslaved and forced ("freed") to build a "home" for the overseers. This home can be described as a single "flying disc" that measures 26,700 miles in circumference. The ship is (was) powered by a Devil (not a demon, but the parent of demons) called Shem... With no lifespan and a home with an unlimited power supply, these overseers extended themselves fully into the physical, where they destroy/hinder any (one/thing/etc.) that they think might empower Elohim further. They have been known to park their home/ship between a planet and

$\longrightarrow$

<-- continued from above

its sun, in order to kill the planet and all who dwell upon it.

These people are, loosely, the origin of the Vril. In fact, they are correctly referred to as Vrillains or Vrillians.

The Vril can also use their home/ship like a huge magnifying glass to concentrate solar energy as a weapon (like frying ants).

They supported C/Kain (with one or two fallout outs) and were part of why he felt so bold.

They are never seen! (Even Mike E. has heard of them as likely to exist, but has never seen them.)

When they venture out of the home ship, they wander through the world like beings of glass…nearly impossible to see and able to "phase" in order to pass through solids – even so far as to allow rain to pass right through them, to avoid detection.

The Vrillains are not the origin of the Nazi

continued ->

←

it's ~~fried~~ Sun, in order to kill the planet and all who dwell upon it.

These people are, loosely, the origin of the Vril. In fact, they are correctly refered to as: Vrillains or Vrillians.

The Vril can also use their home/ship like a huge magnifying glass to concentrate solar energy as a weapon (like frying ants).

They supported c/Kane (with one or two falling ants) and were part of why he felt so bold.

They are never seen ↙ (even Mike E. has heard of them (as likely to exist) but, never seen them.

When they venture out of the home ship, they wander through the world like beings of glass... nearly impossible to see and able to "phase" in order to pass through solids — even so far as to allow rain to pass right through them, to avoid detection.

The Vrillains are not the origin of the Nazi
→

<-- continued from above

Frozen "Ice" Universe Theory. That came from a misunderstood document from the end of an Ice Age (As a man was trying to describe the "human evidence" (tools, constructions, etc.) that were appearing as the ice melted away…even creatures that seemed to come back to life, after being trapped in the ice.).

Since the Vrillains miscalculated the whole experiment, they now get to face their own version of it: To have "everything" only to lose it and have to start over. How perfect will Their bodies and form seem now, in their artificial, and now powerless, home/ship. Be careful what you ask for!

It's a revers version of the experiment: We started the experiment with nothing and are working our way toward everything. While they started with everything and abused it until it was gone.

They saw Elohim as The Enemy, as a threat to their own power. They never imagined that the most terrifying creature of all was the one who wants none of it, none of what they have or had.

continued ->

←

Frozen "Ice" Universe Theory — That came from a misunderstood document from the end of an Ice Age (As a man was trying to describe the "human evidence" (tools, constructions, etc.) that were appearing as the ice melted away... even creatures that seemed to come back to life, after being trapped in the ice.

Since The Vrillains miscalculated the whole experiment, they now get to face their own version of it: To have "everything" only to lose it and have to start over. How perfect will their bodies and form seem now, in their artificial, and now powerless, home/ship. Be careful what you ask for!

It's a reverse version of the experiment: We started the experiment with nothing, and are working our way toward everything. While they started with everything, and abused it until it was gone.

They saw Elohim as The enemy, as a threat to their own power. They never imagined that the most terrifying creature of all, was The one who wants none of it, none of what they have or had.

⟶

<-- continued from above

The lesson that matters is this: The Vrillains are part of our true, original world. In working so hard to destroy a single perceived threat ("enemy") they opened themselves up to total conquest by one that they did not even see or imagine. They did not believe in Death, until Death came for Them.

Absolutes are inescapable, absolutely!

- ST   (Symbol)   (Symbol)

"Poem"

The Dragon holds the Pearl in his hand
The Pearl is Everything, including the Dragon
The Dragon is Everything, including the Pearl
Anything that is neither the Pearl nor the Dragon,
   simply is not
That which is not, is also the Dragon, but is not the Pearl
Everything and Nothing are the same only from the
    perspective of the Dragon

            -ST

            continued ->

←

The lesson that matters is this: The Villains are part of our true, original, world. In working so hard to destroy a single perceived threat ("enemy") they opened themselves up to total conquest by one that they did not even see or imagine. They did not believe in Death, until Death came for them.

Absolutes are inescapable, absolutely!

$ △ ☉/TJ

The Dragon holds the Pearl in his hand
The Pearl is Everything, including the Dragon
The Dragon is Everything, including the Pearl
Anything that is neither the Pearl nor the Dragon,
    simply is not.
That which is not, is also the Dragon, but is not the Pearl
Everything and Nothing are the same only from the
    perspective of the Dragon

$

→

<-- continued from above

Regarding the "Poem:"

Eve asked me, "If I am in the Pearl and you are the Dragon, and you (the Dragon) are also in the Pearl ... then that creates an infinity loop (∞), and that I do understand. But, if everything is in the infinity loop, then what is Nothing...what is that which is outside the loop of infinity?"

I explained that if the infinity loop is visualized as an hourglass, then all things and all dimensions dwell within that hourglass. This speaks of the hour-glass itself, not of the empty space within it, nor what is not within it, but rather beyond it. The hourglass, itself, is everything...infinite and forever...truly everything (heaven, earth, thought, etc.). What is not dwells within the hourglass and beyond the hourglass, and can represent the infinitely and forever Large, and the infinitely and forever Small. Still, everything is in the hourglass...whatever dwells within or beyond the hourglass Is Not. As with "Silence" there is more that is not, then there actually Is. And, what is...Is Infinite, Is Everything, Is What Is!

continued ->

←

Regarding The "Poem":

Eve asked me, "If I am in the Pearl and you are the Dragon, and you (the Dragon) are also in the Pearl... Then that creates an infinity loop (∞), and that I do understand. But, if everything is in the infinity loop, then what is Nothing... what is that which is outside the loop of infinity?"

I explained that if the infinity loop is visualized as an hour-glass, then all things and all dimensions dwell within that hour-glass. This speaks of the hour-glass itself, not of the empty space within it, nor what is not within it, but rather beyond it. The hour-glass, itself, is everything... infinite and forever... truly everything (heaven, earth, thought, etc.). What is not dwells within the hourglass and beyond the hour-glass, and can represent the infinitely and forever large, and the infinitely and forever small. Still, everything is the hour-glass... whatever dwells within or beyond the hour-glass Is Not. As with "Silence" there is more that is not, than there actually is. And, what is... Is Infinite, Is Everything, Is What Is !

⟶

<-- continued from above

Even that which we call the "physical," AKA E's den, is just a bump in the surface of the glass, on the inside (headed toward "small") that the Serpent called E found while looking for someplace quiet to rest. The overly exploratory E just ventured a bit beyond what was and the "den" he found (created)…that little bump on the glass…is what we call the Universe, Multiverse, etc. Even Elohim's "Kingdom" (AKA Heaven) is only a tiny step back toward the greater eternal everything that is, in this example, the hourglass.

In the universe I described, where everything and forever are the hourglass, it becomes clear how much room there is for us to grow. We need only find the desire to do so, as demonstrated by E and his quest for a den that ultimately made an infinite eternal universe just a little bit bigger.

-ST

Even that which we call the "physical", AKA E's den is just a bump in the surface of the glass, on the inside (headed toward "small") that the Serpent called E found while looking for someplace quiet to rest. The overly exploratory E just ventured a bit beyond what was and the "den" he found (created)... that little bump on the glass... is what we call the Universe, multiverse, etc. Even Elohim's "Kingdom" (AKA Heaven) is only a tiny step back toward the greater eternal everything that is, in this example, the hour-glass.

In the universe I described, where everything and forever are the hour-glass, it becomes clear how much room there is for us to grow. We need only find the desire to do so, as demonstrated by E and his quest for a den that ultimately made an infinite eternal universe just a little bit bigger.

Curses 10 Nov 1958

The Smithsonian accepts the Hope Diamond, on behalf of all of the people of The United States of America.

From that day onward, the curse of the Hope is on Lady Liberty and her People.

Y says: That moment was the Peak, everything has been on the decline ever since that moment.

The greatest freest moment of US history was that moment just before the USA accepted ownership/possession of the Hope Diamond.

(Symbol)   -ST

21 Dec 2015:

Fix it!?!? … Fixed!!!

Note: The Hope curse must always be, at least, 80' (feet) away when engaging the "Lemurian" computer program.

(Symbol)

10 Nov 1958

The Smithsonian accepts the Hope Diamond, on behalf of all of the people of the United States of America. From that day onward, the curse of the Hope is on Lady Liberty and her people.

Y says: That moment was the Peak, everything has been on the decline ever since that moment. The greatest freest moment of US history was that moment just before the USA accepted ownership / possession of the Hope Diamond.

△ $

21 Dec. 2015: ~~####~~
    Fix it !?!? ... Fixed !!!

    Note: The Hope curse must always be, at least, 80' away when engaging the "Lemurian" computer program.

Lemurian (Symbol) Machine

(Diagram)

(Remember the Carpet and the Chair)

⌐Lemurian —#— Machine⌐

┤(16)├

(9)
(20)/18
[C]
(10)
(12)   (11)
(22)   (1)
(8)[D](4)   (2)/R1=S1   (3)[A](7)
              R2=S1
(5)   (21)
       (15) (17) (14)
             [B]
             (6)
(13)   (19)

(Remember: The Carpet, and The Chair)

=( )= · A.C.B.

A · Commando (Crook) (2550)
B · Pygmy (Phurba) (--)
C · Midget (E.V.E.) (--)
D · Punisher (Flail) (2500)
R1 · Ruby (P.S.)
R2 · Ruby (P.S)
S1 · Sapphire (E.F.)
1 · Ada (Q)
2 · Flawless 3" (white)
3 · Lemurian
4 · 4 – 6 (Q)
5 · Madagascar
6 · South Africa (Red)
7 · Red Aventurine
8 · Miriam Jasper (Himalaya Sea Bed)
9 · Red "Malachite" Jasper
10 · Shungite (Black)
11 · Storm Jade (Old)
12 · Storm Jade (New)
13 · Fluorite (Purple)
14 · Citrine Tibet (Yellow)
15 · Yellow Quartz
16 · Gift (From Raven (special)
17 · Blue Opal (Peru)
18 · Ruby Zoisite (Thor's Hammer)
19 · Geode (Lace Agate) (MT)
20 · Meteorite (Tibet) (Dragon Skull)
21 · Pyrite (skull)
22 · White Jade

=()= • A.C.B.

A • Commando (Crook) (2550)
B • Pygmy (Phurba) (—)
C • Midget (E.V.E.) (—)
D • Punisher (Flail) (2500)
R1 • Ruby (P.S.)
R2 • Ruby (P.S.)
S1 • Sapphire (E.F.)

1 • Ada (Q)
2 • Flawless 3" (white)
3 • Lemurian
4 • 4-6 (Q)
5 • Madagascar
6 • South Africa (Red)
7 • Red Adventurine
8 • Miriam Jasper (Himalaya / Sea Bed)
9 • Red "Malachite" Jasper
10 • Shungite (Black)
11 • Storm Jade (old)
12 • Storm Jade (New)
13 • Fluorite (Purple)
14 • Citrine Tibet (yellow)
15 • Yellow Quartz
16 • Gift (From Raven) (special)
17 • Blue Opal (Peru)
18 • Ruby Zoisite (Thor's Hammer)
19 • Geode (Lace Agate) (14)
20 • Meteorite (Tibet) (Dragon Skull)
21 • Pyrite (Skull)
22 • White Jade

Place · Carpet and Chair (wood)

Place · Triangle

Place · 2, swords, 18/20 (Plus: R1, R2, S1)

Connect · Each sword to 20 (clockwise) (Midget First)

Connect · 2 to 18, then 18 to 20

Place · Skulls (clockwise) (Shungite First)

Connect · Power (clockwise)

Connect · Opposites

Connect · 1- off (clockwise)

Connect · 2 – off (clockwise)

Connect · 3 off (clockwise)

Connect · 4 off (clockwise)

Connect · 5 off (clockwise)

S
I { 9 Replaces 20/18, while 20/18 rotate inward (colckwise3)
T

Connect · Guards (circumphrally)

Allow to Run (80 minutes) (Leave Everything As It Is)

20/18 Rotate Outward, then Remove 18/20 (counter clockwise3, then lift)

Remove · Guards (clockwise, 9 is last)

Remove · Swords (clockwise, C is last)

Dismantle: Starting w/11

Remove · Power

Remove · Triangle

Remove · 2 (R1, R2, S1)

Remove · Chair

Remove · Carpet

Place · Carpet and Chair (wood)
Place · Triangle
Place · 2, swords, 18/20 (Plus: R1, R2, S1)
Connect · Each Sword to 20 (clockwise) (midget First)
Connect · 2 to 18, then 18 to 20
Place · Skulls (clockwise) (shungite First)
Connect · Power (clockwise)
Connect · Oposites
Connect · 1-off (clockwise)
Connect · 2-off (clockwise)
Connect · 3 off (clockwise)
Connect · 4 off (clockwise)
Connect · 5 off (clockwise)

S {
I
T {

9 Replaces 20/18, while 20/18 rotate inward (clockwise)
Connect · Guards (circumphrally)
Allow To Run (80 minutes) (Leave Everything As It Is)
20/18 Rotate Outward, then Remove 18/20 (Counter clockwise, They Lift)
Remove · Guards (clockwise, 9 is last)
Remove · Swords (clockwise, C is last)
Dismantle: Starting w/ 11
Remove · Power
Remove · Triangle
Remove · 2 (R1, R2, S1)
Remove · Chair
Remove · Carpet

75

A "weapon" that they tried to use against me.

                                                - It didn't work

World Seed

A divine plant, from the place of our origin, that, when placed in a positive environment, will grow, like a leafless tree. Each plant, or tree, is a singular plane (dimension) but, when many are planted together in the same area/place, then what grows is a forest of singular planes (dimensions).

When one walks through such a forest one can encounter one tree or many trees, as they grow and become intertwined. To walk through such a forest is to move between dimensions; at times existing in many, and at other times just a few, or even one or none at all.

That you are, and that you are walking, is the only truth of such a forest … the rest is just the trees. What you perceive or see is just that which truly is (you) trying to make sense of what is being experienced; Like dreams, in a strange, foreign and ever changing forest.

                                                             continued ->

A "weapon" that they tried to use against me.
— it didn't work

World Seed

A divine plant, from the place of our origin, that, when placed in a positive environment, will grow, like a leafless tree. Each plant, or tree, is a singular plane (dimension) but, when many are planted together in the same area/place then what grows is a forest of singular planes (dimensions).

When one walks through such a forest one can encounter one tree or many trees, as they grow and become intertwined. To walk through such a forest is to move between dimensions; at times existing in many, and at other times just a few, or even one or none at all.

That you are, and that you are walking is the only truth of such a forest... The rest is just the trees. What you perceive or see is just that which truly is (you) trying to make sense of what is being experienced; Like dreams, in a strange, foreign and ever changing forest.

⟶

<-- continued from above

These seeds are ethereal white balls, like a fluffy dandelion cluster that is blurred until no single shape is visible.

The trees are "oil slick" (every color) black, leafless, flowing surface with long (wild oak) like branches.

(Symbol) Seed   (Symbol) Tree

As these trees intersect they grow into each other, creating intersections of multi-dimensional matter. When they touch, they are one. Like a collective of individual unique dimensions, gaining strength and support by touching (holding hands) with the others.

←

These seeds are etheral white balls, like a fluffy dandelion cluster that is blurred until no single shape is visible.
The trees are "oil slick" (every color) black, leafless, flowing surface with long (wild oak) like branches.

        Seed   Tree

As these trees intersect they grow into each other, creating intersections of multi-dimensional matter. When they touch, they are one. Like a collective of individual unique dimensions, gaining strength and support by touching (holding hands) with the others.

A Year in the Life ...

    Earth: 24 hour day / 365.25 day year
    Solar System: 26,000 year "day"
        226,000,000 year "year"
        8,692.307 "days" per year

One solar system (SS) year ago, Pangea was just beginning to break apart.

The 26,000 year "day" is just that … a day.
The days have night and day, with variation.

The Geological record shows the 26,000 year "day" cycle.

There are also corollaries to the earth seasons: Fall, Winter, Spring and Summer…Though, we do not know how many seasons there are in our SS year. Nor do we know how such seasons actually vary.

Everything in our Galaxy, and its proximity to us, has an effect. Kinda like astrology or tides.

Night vs Day length varies through the SS year. Advanced life, as we know it, is only within the past SS year.

                                        continued ->

A year in the life...

Earth: 24 hour day / 365.25 day year
Solar System: 26,000 year "day"
        226,000,000 year "year"
        8,692.307 "days" per year

One solar system (SS) year ago Pangea was just beginning to break apart.

The 26,000 year "day" is just that... a Day.
    The days have night and day, with variation.

The Geological record shows the 26,000 year "day" cycle.

There are also corelaries to the earth seasons: Fall, Winter, Spring and Summer... Though, we do not know how many seasons there are in our SS year. Nor do we know how such seasons actually vary.

Everything in our Galaxy, and its proximity to us, has an effect. Kinda like astrology or tides.

Night vs Day length varries through the SS year. Advanced life, as we know it, is only within the past SS year.   ⟶

<-- continued from above

Pre-2 SS years ago: only multi-cell organisms.

About 2 SS years ago: First life w/shells and invertebrates.

Over the next SS year:
    Fish develop (490 mya)
    Plants move to land (443 mya)
    Insects develop (417 mya) – then move to land
    Amphibians dominate (354 mya)
    Reptiles develop (323 mya)
    Triassic – Dinosaurs take over (248 mya)
    "Birds" appear (206 mya)
    First flower plants (144 mya)
    Dinosaurs extinct (as if!) (65 mya)
    Mammals took over Thereafter

Humans (us) have been around for just 49 SS days.

Note: Dinosaurs rule for 180 million years. Then winter hits and the mammals took over.

←

Pre-2 SS years ago: only multi-cell organisms.

About 2 SS years ago: First life w/ shells and invertabrates.

Over the next SS year:
  Fish develop (490 mya)
  Plants move to land (443 mya)
  Insects develop (417 mya) - then move to land
  Amphibeans dominate (354 mya)
  Reptiles develop (323 mya)
  Triassic - Dinosaurs take over (248 mya)
  "Birds" appear (206 mya)
  First flowering plants (144 mya)
  Dinosaurs extinct (as if!) (65 mya)
  Mamals took over thereafter

Humans (us) have been around for just 49 SS days.

Note: Dinosaurs rule for 180 million years, then winter hits and the mamals took over.

22 June 2016   +/- 4 pm Pacific Time

(Symbol)

(symbol)

Rise and fall in opposite unison – always keeping the "loop" at the same "circle" diameter at the bottom.

Seemed to flow, rather than fly, almost with the wind, except that it followed the driveway uphill, always maintaining 4 – 5 foot altitude.

It turned to change "focus" of the loop and then turned back (as if noticing that I was looking at it) and then "took off" at a steep climb to head up hill and over the trees.

I could not place the shape at the time, but each lobe looked like a small Scandinavian puku knife.

22 June 2016   +/- 4pm Pacific Time

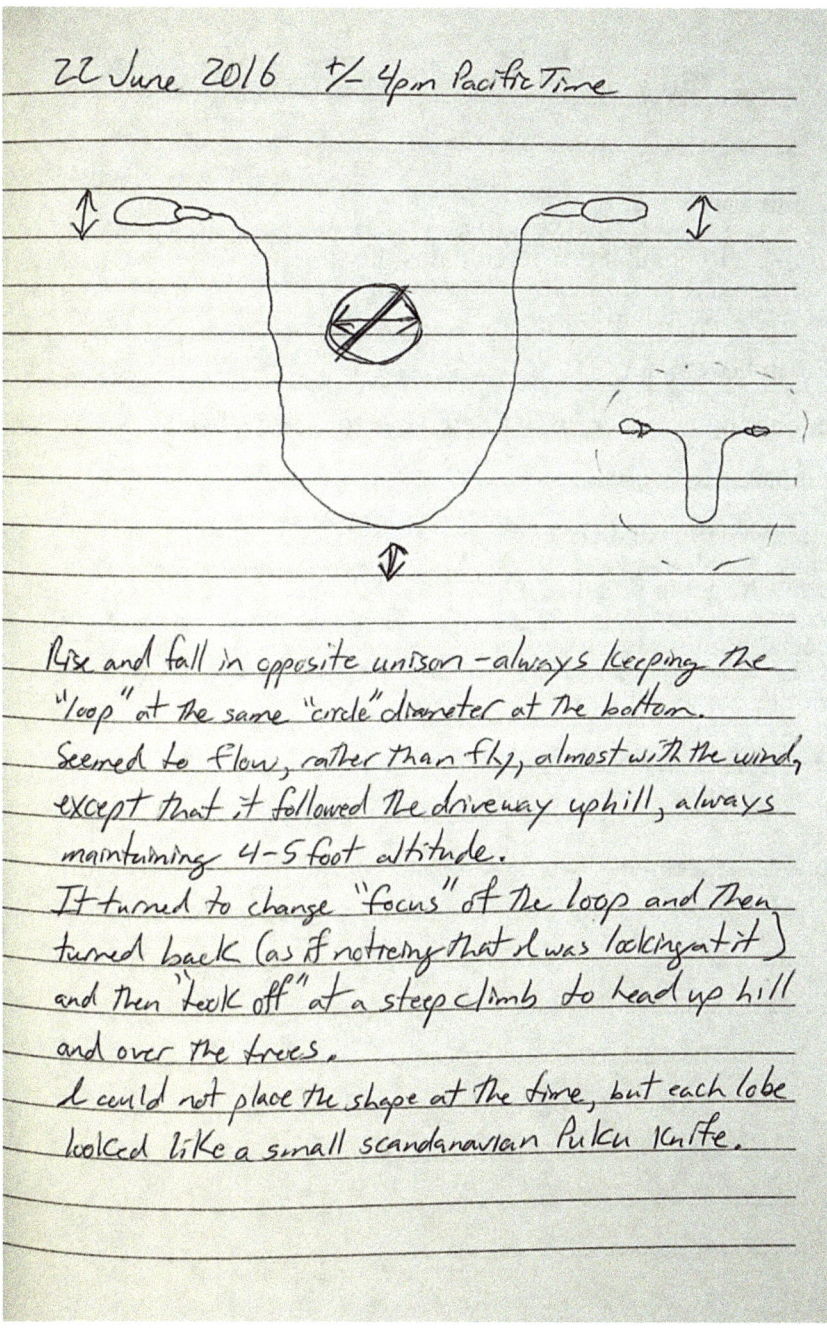

Rise and fall in opposite unison — always keeping the "loop" at the same "circle" diameter at the bottom. Seemed to flow, rather than fly, almost with the wind, except that it followed the driveway uphill, always maintaining 4-5 foot altitude.
It turned to change "focus" of the loop and then turned back (as if noticing that I was looking at it) and then "took off" at a steep climb to head up hill and over the trees.
I could not place the shape at the time, but each lobe looked like a small scandanavian Puku knife.

A Simple Elixir   NF

Life, in holy water (3)

Yami-12, to break it down (contains the fire)

Time, in sacred honey

Life, in holy water (3)

Healing light (3x1 or 1x3), filtered by stone and silver

God bless us, every one

Clean the stone and silver

"Don't forget to breathe"

Cheers, bottoms up

Be quiet for a moment   (symbol)

Live long and prosper

Note: One becomes Two in Alabaster vessel (if blessed by him)

A Simple Elixer   NF

Life, in holy water (3)
Yami-12, to break it down (contains the fire)
Time, in sacred honey
Life, in holy water (3)
Healing light (3×1 or 1×3), filtered by stone and silver
God bless us, every one
Clean the stone and silver
"Don't forget to breathe"
Cheers, bottoms up
Be quiet for a moment
Live long and prosper

Note: One becomes Two in Alabaster vessel (if blessed by him)

Color Plates

Plate 1

Plate 2

Plate 3

Plate 4

Plate 5

Plate 6

Plate 7

Plate 8

Plate 9

Plate 10

Plate 11

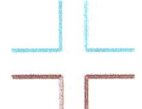

Healing Device (Symbol)

Filter + Regulate Rubic + Sapphiric energy for health and healing

(Symbol)   est. 1' square cube transparent quartz
"White"
Other shapes work as well.

a – 8mm Red
b – empty
c – 8mm Red
d – 8mm Blue or Red
e – 9 mm Red
f – 8mm Red

Red is · Rubic Energy · Ruby
Blue is · Sapphiric Energy · Blue Sapphire
} All corundum connects to sapphiric energy.

Sapphiric energy is "Transformative."

· Red, White, Blue devices: Always more white (quartz) then Red (Ruby) and B (Blue Sapphire), combined.

Always more Red than Blue, even if there is no Blue.

continued ->

THD

Healing Device

Filter + Regulate Rubic + Sapphiric energy for health and healing

est. 1" square cube transparent quartz "White"

Other shapes work as well.

a – 8mm Red
b – empty
c – 8mm Red
d – 8mm Blue or Red
e – 8mm Red
f – 8mm Red

Red is • Rubic Energy • Ruby
Blue is • Sapphiric Energy • Blue Sapphire

{ All Corundum connects to sapphiric energy. }

Sapphiric energy is "Transformative".

• Red, white, Blue devices: Always more white (quartz) Then Red (Ruby) and B (Blue Sapphire), combined. Always more Red than Blue, even if there is no Blue.

⟶

<-- continued from above

Transformative Energy (TE)

The Transformative Energy that can be drawn out of ruby or sapphire comes from a singular dimension, which contains only an infinite universe of Transformative Energy.

TE can be drawn to our universe (dimension) from the dimension of Sapphiric Energy by drawing it out of Ruby and/or Sapphire by use of direct contact with quartz.

The TE that is drawn to us through corundum, aka Ruby, aka Sapphire, is referred to as "Sapphiric Energy."

All Sapphiric Energy is Transformative, but not all Transformative Energy is Sapphiric.

Quartz is a "Transformer"

Quartz transforms the TE source to a detectable and/or usable type of energy.

Ruby and Sapphire are the window/doorway from the Human Centric Dimensions (HCD) to the Eternal and Infinite dimension, or sea, of Transformative Energy.

TE transfer generates no detectable Thermal output!

continued ->

←

Transformative Energy (TE)

The Transformative Energy that can be drawn out of ruby or sapphire comes from a singular dimension, which contains only an infinite universe of Transformative Energy.

TE can be drawn to our universe (dimensions) from the dimension of Sapphiric Energy by drawing it out of Ruby and/or Sapphire by use of direct contact with quartz.

The TE that is drawn to us through Corundum aka Ruby aka Sapphire is refered to as Sapphiric Energy.

All Sapphiric Energy is Transformative, but not all Transformative Energy is Sapphiric.

Quartz is a "Transformer"
Quartz transforms the TE source to a detectable and/or usable type of Energy.

Ruby and Sapphire are the window/doorway from the Human Centric Dimensions (HCD) to the Eternal and Infinite dimension, or sea, of Transformative Energy.

TE transfer generates no detectable Thermal output!

⟶

<-- continued from above

Direct physical contact with Quartz draws the TE, from its place of origin, into the HCD where it may be detected, and harnessed for use, as it does, in a say, represent the potential to do work.

The TE, once drawn into the HCD, will immediately begin flowing/filtering back to its point of origin. The result is that no amount, great or small, of TE drawn from the Sapphiric Sea ever actually represents any amount at all, relative to the infinite sea from whence it came. $\infty - x = \infty$ (always)

Since the TE returns to the TE Sea, naturally from the HCD, without any outside influence or process, the flow of TE, sapphic or otherwise, represents an inexhaustible source of usable energy. It is self-replenishing energy that is infinite and may never be destroyed or created … only harnessed and used.

It is like water, a consumable that is, for all intents and purposes, just being moved around. Also, like water, it is beneficial to most, simply by its presence and, if you can figure out how to harness it, it can be used to provide energy (do work) on an infinite scale, forever.

continued ->

Direct physical contact with Quartz draws the TE, from its place of origin, into the HCD where it may be detected, and harnessed for use, as it does, in a way, represent the potential to do work.

The TE, once drawn into the HCD, will imediately begin flowing/filtering back to its point of origin. The result is that no amount, great or small, of TE drawn from the Sapphiric Sea ever actually represents any amount at all, relitive to the infinite sea from whence it came. $\infty - x = \infty$ (always)

Since the TE returns to the TE Sea, naturally, from the HCD, without any outside influence or process, the flow of TE, sapphiric or otherwise, represents an inexaustable source of usable energy. It is self-replenishing energy that is infinite and may never be destroyed or created ... only harnessed and used.

It is like water, a consumable that is, for all intents and purposes, just being moved around. Also, like water, it is beneficial to most, simply by its presence and, if you can figure out how to harness it, it can be used to provide energy (do work) on an infinite scale, forever.

<-- continued from above

The Blue Sapphire acts as an alternate flow, which has the effect of regulating the otherwise uncontrolled flow of TE when both the Ruby and Sapphire are touching the quartz.

If only a Ruby and Quartz are use, the TE that draws out is much more Raw and Uncontrolled.

Think of it like Chi: Everyone has Chi flowing, like the Ruby. But, introduce a Master to regulate the flow and the chi will be much more useful.

Think of the Sapphire as a flow regulating plug in a hose or fuel line, or as a "Transistor."

Al_2O_3: Until the Aluminum Oxide is contaminated sufficiently, the flow of TE cannot begin. There must be contaminants to provide the "Gravity" to start the flow (to prime the pump, as it were) through the proverbial hose that is the Ruby or Sapphire.

Pure, uncontaminated Al_2O_3 will not "flow" TE to the HCD, but rather it naturally draws TE from the HCD and "returns" it to the TE dimension.

The Blue Sapphire acts as an alternate flow, which has the effect of regulating, the otherwise uncontrolled, flow of TE when both the Ruby and Sapphire are touching the quartz.

If only a Ruby and Quartz are used, the TE that draws out is much more Raw and Uncontrolled.

Think of it like Chi: Everyone has chi flowing, like the Ruby. But, introduce a Master to regulate the flow and the Chi will be much more useful.

Think of the Sapphire as a flow regulating plug in a hose or fuel line, or as a "Transistor."

Al_2O_3: Until the Aluminum Oxide is contaminated sufficiently the flow of TE cannot begin. There must be contaminants to provide the "Gravity" to start the flow (to prime the pump, as it were) through the proverbial hose that is the Ruby or Sapphire.

Pure, uncontaminated Al_2O_3 will not "flow" TE to the HCD, but rather it naturally draws TE from the HCD and "returns" it to the TE dimension.

E's Den

As we move closer to home, the pillar will slowly expand until it literally fills the magic circle. In a manner of speaking, when the hole is plugged, the door will close.

14 Oct. 2016 @ 10:23 am Pacific Time

Ceremony: Confirmation and acceptance of the Gift.

As the ceremony ended, the pillar sealed the circle. Now, as the last of us trickle out, the importance of the seal is that it protects us from the outside influences (the various things that saw the destruction of the creature as an opportunity).

It is the beginning of the post-biblical era, we just happen to still be here, for a while. From here on out, it is all on them.

-ST

The world is at an end, but the World of Man is only just beginning. What comes next is the grand experiment

E's den — as we move closer to home, the pillar will slowly expand until it literally fills the magic circle. In a maner of speaking, when the hole is plugged, the door will close.

14 Oct. 2016 @ 10:23am Pacific Time
Ceremony: Confirmation and acceptance of the Gift. As the ceremony ended, the pillar sealed the circle. Now, as the last of us trickle out, the importance of the seal is that it protects us from the outside influences (the various things that saw the destruction of the creature as an oportunity).

It is the beginning of the post-biblical era, we just happen to still be here, for a while. From here on out, it is all on them. $

The world is at an end, but the world of Man is only just beginning. What comes next is the grand experiment.

The End & The Beginning

2354: It begins! A rapid onset ice age for all of the Earth. Onset will take only 10 – 13 years

2367: Fully immersed in a global ice age

2368: 95% of all humans, on Earth, have died.

2388: 98% of the pre-ice age human population, on Earth, have died.

2400: World population is 1% of the pre-ice age number. Of that remaining population, 90% are "Americans" (What would today, 2017, be considered the USA). Only 10% are comprised of any non-USA American people. The 10% includes every non-American, including Canada, Mexico, etc.

Thank God for Kansas, and for quality axes!

Some go high, some go low, but everyone dies.

-ST

The End + The Beginning

2354: It begins! A rapid onset ice age for all of the Earth.
Onset will take only 10-13 years.

2367: Fully immersed in a global ice age.

2368: 95% of all humans, on Earth, have died.

2388: 98% of the pre-iceage human population, on Earth, have died.

2400: World population is 1% of the pre-iceage number. Of that remaining population, 90% are "Americans". (what would today, 2017, be considered the USA). Only 10% are comprised of any non-USA American people. The 10% includes every non-American, including Canada, Mexico, etc.

Thank God for Kansas, and for quality axes!

Some go high, some go low, but everyone dies.

The Ark

The man who carries the Ark before him, is invincible.

The army which carries the Ark before it, is that man's.

No population shall ever be worth. However, if they serve the worthy man, they will be victorious.

Men built it into existence, one man will carry it home. Men have lived and died by its power, one man eats its power to live, so that others may die. Death is God, Dragon is King.

There is a Yin and a Yang to the grand experiment. If our goal was to grow, to become more than we were, the goal of men is to do the same, to become more than they were, or ever could be without a push in the right direction. But, we needed a push too, and it was they who provided it (limitation).

Without us, there would be no future for man.
Unless we leave, the future will not be theirs.

continued ->

The Ark

The man who carries the Ark before him,
is invincible.
The army which carries the Ark before it, is
that man's.
No population shall ever be worthy. However,
if they serve the worthy man, they will be victorious.

Men built it into existance, one man will carry
it home. Men have lived and died by its power,
one man eats its power to live, so that others may
die. Death is God, Dragon is King.

There is a Yin and a Yang to the grand experiment.
If our goal was to grow, to become more than we were.
The goal of men is to do the same, to become more
than they were, or ever could be without a push in
the right direction. But, we needed a push too, and
it was they who provided it (limitation)

Without us, there would be no future for man.
Unless we leave, the future will not be theirs.

⟶

<-- continued from above

    The Ark shall guide us home.

    The trumpet shall sound us on.

    What we leave behind is everything,

    What we take with us is so much more.

The End

Now, we stir the pot. When we stop, we will finally see what we have created.

When nature calls them, what remains will truly be theirs.

-ST

←

The Ark shall guide us home.
The trumpet shall sound us on.

What we leave behind is everything,
what we take with us is so much more.

The End

Now, we stir the pot. When we stop, we will finally see what we have created.

When nature calls them, what remains will truly be theirs.

do not dwell upon what you can do
do what must be done
as long as infinite souls dwell within our hears
the only limit to what we can do
is what we are willing to do
it is a double-edged sword

- XU

(Redacted)

continued ->

do not dwell upon what you can do
do what must be done
as long as infinite souls dwell within our hearts
the only limit to what we can do
is what we are willing to do
it is a double edged sword

─xu

Nephilim

3 Dec 2017

(Symbol) - Paris - Argentina - (Symbol)

There were four Nephilim in the world of men, as we entered the 21st century.

With the death of Caine, they recognized that the world of men would soon end (as they know it).

The remaining Nephilim divide the world in parts, each controls one point on the compass. N, S, E, W.

N & S are Poles, while E & W are the centers of the great seas at the equator. The net effect is that no single Nephilim is over any one part of the earth. They overlap, that way they can keep an eye on each other.

The work that I have been doing is getting too close to these rulers, and they are becoming nervous. On the 3rd of December in 2017, the South Carolina Nephilim struck me. Seeing my focus was on a traveler, the Nephilim or White Night struck me directly. Its form was not able to detectably contact my physical body (that I could tell) but it did contact (Physically) many parts within my body. Most notably, it knocked out a temporary crown on the upper right side of my mouth. If I had not been lucky enough to have a part of my body that contained a material that the Nephilim could physically touch …

continued ->

3 Dec 2017

(Prague) - Paris - Argentina - (S.C.)

There were four Nephilim in the world of men, as we entered the 21st century.

With the death of Caine they recognized that the world of men would soon end (as they know it)

The remaining Nephilim divide the world in parts, each controls one point on the compass. N, S, E, W. N+S are Poles, while E+W are the centers of the great seas at the equator. The net effect is that no single Nephilim is over any one part of the earth. They overlap, that way they can keep an eye on each other.

The work that I have been doing is getting too close to these rulers, and they are becoming nervous. On the 3rd of December in 2017, the South Carolina Nephilim struck me. Seeing my focus was on a traveller, the Nephilim or white Alight struck me directly. It's form was not able to detectably contact my physical body (that I could tell) but it did contact (physically) many parts within my body. Most notably, it knocked out a temporary crown on the upper right side of my mouth. If I had not been lucky enough to have a part of my body that contained a material that the Nephilim could physically touch...

→

<-- continued from above
… then I might not have realized that I had been attacked, and struck.

Because I did know, my self defense overkill system kicked in…there are now three Nephilim left in the world of man.

The White Night is no more.

This one was a fallen angel whose plight was dire, and whose heart was lost. A sorry soul, if you could even call it that … so corrupted … so disgusting.

Like silver or the God Killers, the Nephilim can impact some parts of the human reality, in a true physical sense, but they cannot touch everything, or even most of it.

The war to end The Nephilic Plague has begun!

-ST

←

... then I might not have realized that I had been attacked, and struck.

Because I did know, my self defense overkill system kicked in... There are now three Nephilim left in the world of men.

The White Night is no more.

This one was a fallen angel whose plight was dire, and whose heart was lost. A sorry soul, if you could even call it that... so corrupted... so disgusting.

Like silver or the God killers, the Nephilim can impact some parts of the human reality, in a true physical sense, but they cannot touch everything, or even most of it.

The war to end the Nephilic Plague has begun!

Unwritten Word   5 Dec 2017

The Nephilim of Prague was called Unwritten Word. Its ties were deep and intense ... to me and to others. Unwritten Word was the strongest of the remaining Nephilim. It seems, not strong enough.

Both, Unwritten Word and White Night have been undone. They dwell within nothingness, the Trap. Each had an anchor to the created world(s), but their anchors are gone now too.

Of all of the Nephilim, only Argentina and Paris remain. They will hide and plot and pray ... but, only to themselves ... after all, the Curse of the Nephilim is that No One is Listening.

(Symbol)

(Symbol)

(Symbol)

This is the Key to the Nephilim and it will undo the Nephilic Curse or Plague.

Unwritten Word   5 Dec 2017

The Nephilim of Prague was called Unwritten Word. It's ties were deep and intense... to me and to others. Unwritten Word was the strongest of the remaining Nephilim. It seems, not strong enough.

Both, Unwritten Word and White Night have been undone. ~~XXXX~~ They dwell w. Thing no Thingness, the Trap. Each had an anchor to the created world(s), but their anchors are gone now too.

Of all of the Nephilim, only Argentina and Paris remain. They will hide and plot and pray... but, only to themselves... after all, the Curse of Nephilim is that No One Is Listening.

NOIL
7ION

N[O|I]N
[I|O]

This is the Key to Nephilim and it will undo the Nephilic Curse or Plague.

A Poem,

Spells have been cast
Promises have been made
Lost promises destroy spells
No spell destroys promises
Weakness must be overcome
The darkness is light
The light contains darkness
If one becomes two
If two are one
No one shall fall

- The End of the Nephilim

(Symbol)

Two are no more, Only Two remain, The Four will never again ride together, each shall be helpless alone. So it shall be, that it shall no longer be. The end of Nephilim.

A Poem,

Spells have been cast
Promises have been made
Lost promises destroy spells
No spell destroys promises
Weakness must be overcome
The darkness is light
The light contains darkness
If one becomes two
If two are one
No one shall fall

~ The End of Nephilim

```
| 0 | 1 |
| 1 | 0 |
```

Two are no more, Only Two remain, The Four will never again ride together, each shall be helpless alone. So it shall be, That it shall no longer be. The end of Nephilim.

Crystallization, Zyisian

The Cup that contains the crystalized pyramid

The Cup that produces the Obelisk flame

The Box that contains the burning water

The Blades of many things

Rings, Rods, and Wands

Crystallization represents the process of becoming real. That which was not becoming something that actually is.

Through the Zyisian process we coalesce ether into spirit, energy becomes life, potential becomes someone, who is.

Through crystallization we solidify idea, thought becomes substance, vision becomes reality.

One is someone, the other is something.

-ST

What God Did!

Crystalization, Zyisian

The Cup that contains the crystalized pyramid

The Cup that produces the Obelisk flame

The Box that contains the burning water

The Blades of many things

Rings, Rods, and Wands

Crystalization represents the process of becoming real. That which was not becoming something that actually is.

Through the Zyisian process we coalesce ether into spirit, energy becomes life, potential becomes someone, who is.

Through crystalization we solidify idea, Thought becomes substance, vision becomes reality.

One is someone, the other is something.

what God Did !

On Demons, Devils, and Evil Beings

They do not dwell within physical creation by design, any more than we do. That we hold the door open, so that we may experience physical limitation, is how they get here.

They are here because we are here. In the end, we need not drive them out, so that we may leave. But, rather, we must leave, and in doing so we will destroy the mechanism by which they are here.

When the trumpets sound and the lion roars ... when the veil ceases to be ... This will mark the end of our time here, of their time here, of anyone's time here ... save those who are not ... those who are from this place, creation.

No games. No checks, nor balances. Only This one absolute truth ... creation is alone, it is not home to any of us, nor to any who we recognize as being. Creation is only a home to the created, it is Theirs ... forever, or as long as it lasts.

Good and evil are ways, not beings ... the created will be free to choose their own ways ... after we leave.

On Demons, Devils, and Evil Beings

They do not dwell within physical creation by design, any more than we do. That we hold the door open, so that we may experience physical limitation, is how they get here.

They are here because we are here. In the end we need not drive them out, so that we may leave. But, rather we must leave, and in doing so we will destroy the mechanism by which they are here.

When the trumpets sound and the lion roars... when the veil ceases to be... This will mark the end of our time here, of their time here, of any ones time here... save those who are not... those who are from this place, creation.

No games. No checks, nor balances. Only this one absolute truth... creation is alone, it is not home to any of us, nor to any who we recognize as being. Creation is only a home to the created, it is theirs... forever, or as long as it lasts.

Good and evil are ways, not beings... The created will be free to choose their own ways... after we leave.

Solomon

The great king Solomon was, truly, a master of demons. He was the greatest demonologist of his time. Only Princess Honsu, of 21st dynasty Egypt, could even be compared to Solomon's kill, control, and ability.

Solomon instructed two of his sons in demonology. They were instructed at the same time, and each was forbidden to write anything down, while being instructed. Only after they had completed the study, and had spent some time absorbing all that Solomon showed them, could they write any of it down.

In his great wisdom, Solomon had recognized that two people studying the same thing at the same time would recall and record the lessons differently. The truth, or the complete Lesson, would exist somewhere in between the two levels of understanding.

Each version was correct, but together they told the whole story of demonology, from Solomon's view.

Eventually, his two sons did record their versions…

continued ->

Solomon

The great King Solomon was, truly, a master of demons. He was the greatest demonologist of his time. Only Princess Honsu, of 21st dynasty Egypt, could even be compared to Solomon's skill, control, and ability.

Solomon instructed two of his sons in demonology. They were instructed at the same time, and each was forbidden to write anything down, while being instructed. Only after they had completed the study, and had spent some time absorbing all that Solomon showed them, could they write any of it down.

In his great wisdom, Solomon had recognized that two people studying the same thing at the same time would recall and record the lessons differently. The truth, or the complete lesson, would exist somewhere in between the two levels of understanding.

Each vision was correct, but together they told the whole story of demonology, from Solomon's view.

Eventually, his two sons did record their versions...

—>

<-- continued from above

… of what Solomon showed them. One son wrote down his understanding as *Solomon's Key*. This was the *High Key of Solomon*. The other son wrote down his understanding as *Solomon's Jinn*. This was the *Low Key of Solomon*.

The High Key of Solomon focused on how to deal with demons and devils, in the event that you must do so. How to command and control them; how to resist and dismiss them. *Solomon's Key, The High Key of Solomon*, was a wondrous tool for use against demons.

The Low Key of Solomon focused on identifying which demons existed and what each could do for the summoner. Their strengths and abilities; their minions and useful powers. *Solomon's Jinn, The Low Key of Solomon*, was a wondrous catalogue, but less a tool.

The High Key of Solomon still exists today. The most useful examples of the great work are *Mafteah Shelomoh* and *De Nigromancia*. In the forms in which it survives it is still a good and useful work.

The Low Key of Solomon was corrupted, within a …

continued ->

←

... of what Solomon showed them. One son wrote down his understanding as Solomon's Key. This was the High Key of Solomon. The other son wrote down his understanding as Solomon's Jinn. This was the Low Key of Solomon.

The High Key of Solomon focused on how to deal with demons and devils, in the event that you must do so. How to command and control them, how to resist and dismiss them. Solomon's Key, The High Key of Solomon, was a wonderous tool for use against demons.

The Low Key of Solomon focused on identifying which demons existed and what each could do for the summoner. Their strengths and abilities, their minions and useful powers. Solomon's Jinn, The Low Key of Solomon, was a wonderous catalog, but less a tool.

The High Key of Solomon still exists today. The most useful examples of the great work are Mafteah Shelomoh and De Nigromancia. In the forms in which it survives it is still a good and useful work.

The Low Key of Solomon was corrupted, within a ...

→

<-- continued from above

... three generations into something more akin to *The Necronomicon* than most would care to know. Still, *The Low Key of Solomon* also survives, at least in part, as *The Goetia*. There are more complete versions of *The Low Key of Solomon*, the most complete of which exists in a private collection, in France.

Solomon's Key and *Solomon's Jinn*, *The High and Low Keys of Solomon*, are different views of the same teaching. Together they provide the most complete, extant, view of the great secrets and work of the mighty King Solomon.

An interesting side note: H.P. Lovecraft had access to a very good, privately held, version of *Solomon's Jinn*. He used it as a framework to create his own *Necronomicon*. While the names and places have been changed, some of the lesson is still present, some of the power is still there. That is why and how that explains how so many use the "fictional" *Necronomicon* to do real work.

The will and spirit of a magician can create truth from fiction, can create reality from emptiness. Seek only to know and master yourself and you will master everything.

-ST

... Three generations into something more akin to the Necronomicon than most would care to know. Still, the Low Key of Solomon also survives, at least in part, as the Goetia. There are more complete versions of the Low Key of Solomon, the most complete of which exists in a private collection, in France.

Solomon's Key and Solomon's Jinn, the High and Low Keys of Solomon, are different views of the same teaching. Together they provide the most complete, extant, view of the great secrets and work of the mighty king Solomon.

An interesting side note: H.P. Lovecraft had access to a very good, privately held, version of Solomon's Jinn. He used it as a framework to create his own "Necronomicon". While the names and places have been changed some of the lesson is still present, some of the power is still there. That is the why and how that explains how so many use the "fictional" Necronomicon to do real work.

The will and spirit of a magician can create truth from fiction, can create reality from emptiness. Seek only to know and master yourself and you will master everything.

Light Mites and Fallites

Each comes forth from its host as an infinitesimal speck, or dot of pure white energy.

Light Mites do so by direct action/intent, but while directed at a specific target, they do not (require) specific continued focus on the target in order to act.

Fallites do so, seemingly at random, alone or in bunches, as they float out as if dust in air, until they spot their target (evil), then they, or each, dart directly at their evil target. With unwavering, unstoppable perfection they strike.

The effect of Fallites is that they, to evil, are so heavy that any evil they bond to, simply, falls into the earth, as if suddenly influenced by gravity. As the evil falls to the center of the earth, rather than stop falling, the evil falls into "The Trap." Fallites literally cause evil to fall into Hell!

Fallites are the eternal weight of damnation that attaches to evil.

Light Mites are the eternal "drain" of metaphysical energy.

continued ->

Light Mites and Fallites

Each comes forth from its host as an infintecimal speck, or dot of pure white energy.

Light Mites do so by direct action/intent, but while directed at a specific target. They do not specific continued focus on the target in order to act.

Fallites do so, seemingly at random, alone or in bunches, as they float out as if dust in air, until they spot their target (evil), then they, one each, dart directly at their evil target. With unwavering, unstoppable perfection they strike.

The effect of Fallites is that they, to evil, are so heavy that any evil they bond to, simply, falls into the earth, as if suddenly influenced by gravity. As the evil falls to the center of the earth, rather than stop falling, the evil falls into "the Trap". Fallites litterally cause evil to fall into Hell.

Fallites are the eternal weight of damnation that attaches to evil.

Light mites are the eternal "drain" of metaphysical energy.

$\longrightarrow$

<-- continued from above

Fallites: If you are carrying evil, they are the proverbial feather that makes it so heavy that you fall.

Light Mites: If you are attacked, overtly, by someone wielding them, you will be continuously drained of metaphysical energy until they are removed ... good luck with that!

Light Mites: Look sharp and energetic, prickly spheres of energy that can be attached to a weapon or projectile.

Fallites: Look soft and translucent, like light seeds floating in air, until they strike ... so fast!

Fallites: If you are carrying evil, they are the proverbial feather that make it so heavy that you fall.

Lightmites: If you are attacked, overtly, by someone wielding them, you will be continuously drained of metaphysical energy until they are removed... good luck with that!

Light mites: look sharp and energetic, prickley spheres of energy that can be attached to a weapon or projectile.

Fallites: look soft and translucent, like light seeds floating in air, until they strike... so fast!

01 Feb 2017

Breaker of Pacts:

The "pin of pacts" has been destroyed. The blood has been returned.

Yeshua Child

The "chest of souls" has been opened ... in Purgatory.

The "rite of pacts" has been removed, its fire/light still burns, and always shall, but not in the same place, nor for the same person.

No pacts, ever again, for the price of a soul, nor otherwise.

The era of pacts has ended!

(Symbol)

01 Feb. 2017

Breaker of Pacts:

The "pin of pacts" has been destroyed. The blood has returned.

Yeshua Child

The "chest of souls" has been opened... in Purgatory.

The "rite of pacts" has been removed, its fire/light still burns, and always shall, but not in the same place, nor for the same person.

No pacts, ever again, for the price of a soul, nor otherwise.

The era of pacts has ended!

△

The Scroll of A'gypt

To Him I Am

That I Am Is All

I Need To Be

- A'gypt

A'gypt can be considered the founder of what became Egypt, as we know it.

His scroll is the central piece (or cornerstone) of all Egyptian magic and power. It is the written Word, or Magic, of God, floating along through what can be described as the sea. Held down, or anchored, to the sea, in order to keep it from flying away in the wind. Anchored by two deer/stag Antlers, one complete and one with a single broken point, which signified the struggle to bring the scroll into being.

To Him I Am

That I Am Is All

I Need To Be

- A'gypt

The Scroll of A'gypt

>   To Him I Am
> That I Am Is All
>   I Need To Be
>
>   — A'gypt

A'gypt can be considered the founder of what became Egypt, as we know it.

His scroll is the central piece (or cornerstone) of all Egyptian magic and power. It is the written Word, or Magic, of God, floating along through what can be described as the sea. Held down, or anchored, to the sea, in order to keep it from flying away in the wind. Anchored by two deer/stag Antlers, one complete and one with a single broken point, which signified the struggle to bring the scroll into being.

>   To Him I Am
> That I Am Is All
>   I Need To Be
>
>   — A'gypt

The End of Us

2116 =/- 11 years

As the proverbial us fades from physical reality, They (created man) begin to see and detect/measure when and that we exist here. In a classic example of claiming victory and success for other people's work, created man (CM) begins a purification effort, man may attempt to reclaim what is rightfully theirs (physical reality). It is ultimately the moment in history that turns the world against religion and any "celebration" of the proverbial us.

CM, with their new-found ability to detect, not only the metaphysical, but the soul itself, takes a turn toward Holocaust and begins isolating US, and even killing and burning us, in the classic sense of the human witch hunt.

Most of us know, by the twenty-second century, that we have nothing to fear ... even as they destroy us. This, of course, makes them even more afraid of us and the soul.

By 2127 there are none of us left, in the physical, except for the one soul that they simply cannot detect, or live without ... EVE!

This post-soul era can be considered the beginning of the Valliant Thor/Victory 1 era. And, the detectable ...

continued ->

The End of Us

2116 +/- 11 years

As the proverbial us fades from physical reality, they (created man) begin to see and detect/measure when and that we exist here. In a classic example of claiming victory and success for other people's work, created man (cm) begins a purification effort, man may attempt to reclaim what is rightfully theirs (physical reality). It is ultimately this moment in history that turns the world against religion and any "celebration" of the proverbial us. CM, with their new found ability to detect, not only the metaphysical, but the soul itself, takes a turn toward Holocaust and begins isolating us, and even killing and burning us, in the classic sense of the human witch hunt. Most of us know, by the twenty second century, that we have nothing to fear... even as they destroy us. This, of course, makes them even more afraid of us and the soul. By 2127 there are none of us left, in the physical, except for the one soul that they simply cannot detect, or live without... EVE! This post soul era can be considered the beginning of the Valiant Thor / Victory 1 era. And, the detectable...

$\longrightarrow$

<-- continued from above

...soul is ultimately used as justification to eliminate any and all religion as well as forbidding EVE from reproducing.

Of course, that their entire civilization is, ultimately, dependent upon EVE and that they never develop the ability to match and/or replace her is lost on most. But for those who "get it," EVE becomes the example of the existence of the "divine" and the motivation to keep religion alive, in secret and otherwise.

Watching us marched to our deaths and the world purged of souls by fire is/was quite unnerving. Seeing the sheep contracting the divine in order to claim adulthood and put their own fingerprint on physical reality is overwhelming, and sad.

It is through this period of "eliminating the parents" that CM empowers themselves, by changing who and what they are. They transform humanity into the "Greys" of UFO conspiracy fame. This happens slowly, at first, but about 200 years post-us, the weather changes and the "Die off of '95" ultimately seals CM's fate as the "Greys." The virtual elimination and/or isolation of anything perceived as being that of Divine Man or our metaphysical reality ...They move on, and rarely look back.

... soul is ultimately used as justification to eliminate any and all religion as well as forbidding EVE from reproducing. Of course, that their entire civilization is, ultimately, dependent upon EVE and that they never develop the ability to match and/or replace her is lost on most. But, for those who "get it", EVE becomes the example of the existence of the "divine" and the motivation to keep religion alive, in secret and otherwise.

Watching us marched to our deaths and the world purge of souls by fire is/was quite unnerving. Seeing the sheep contradicting the divine in order to claim adulthood and put their own fingerprint on physical reality is overwhelming, and sad. It is through this period of "eliminating the parents" that CM empowers themselves, by changing who and what they are. They transform humanity into the "Greys" of UFO conspiracy fame. This happens slowly, at first, but about 200 years post us, the weather changes and the "Die off of 95" ultimately seals CM's fate as the "Greys"; the virtual elimination and/or isolation of anything perceived as being that of Divine Mom or our metaphysical reality.... They move on, and rarely look back.

Anubis, Yin, Yang, Witches, Tengu

Anubis grabbed my attention; he warned me that something, or someone, was coming, in the next 48 hours ... Cataclysmic! I would be needed in two days.

Yin & Yang grabbed my attention; except that it was not actually them ... rather, it was "the witches." They had overpowered the presence of Yin & Yang:

The Witches were chanting a story at me, to draw me into the story that Anubis had shared, but creating a sense that it was an evil, that I should stop. But No!

The Witches are the ones in danger from what comes at this time. They just hoped that I would save them from it.

I trapped many witches and I trapped a horcrux, that was in a Japanese Katana – the sword belonged to the Queen witch ... it was still "H" ... at least it was, as of last night.

I sought out the stone through Oni giant and his Tengu friend. The Tengu was nowhere to be found and the Giant was cocooned in white binding silk. I freed the giant and then the Tengu appeared. The Tengu was hiding from the witches, it was they who trapped the giant, tor protect the queen.

continued ->

Anubis, Yin, Yang, Witches, Tengu

Anubis grabbed my attention; he warned me that something, or someone, was coming, in the next 48 hours... cataclysmic! I would be needed in two days.

Yin + Yang grabbed my attention; except that it was not actually them... rather, it was "The Witches". They had overpowered the presence of Yin + Yang: The Witches were chanting a story at me, to draw me into the story that Anubis had shared, but creating a sense that it was an evil, that I should stop. But No! The Witches are the ones in danger from what comes at this time. They just hoped that I would save them from it.

I trapped many witches and I trapped a horcrux, that was in a Japanese Katana — the sword belonged to the Queen witch... it was still "H"... at least it was, as of last night.

I sought out the stone throwing Oni giant and his Tengu friend. The Tengu was nowhere to be found and the giant was cocooned in white binding silk. I freed the giant and then the Tengu appeared. The Tengu was hiding from the witches, it was they who trapped the giant, to protect the queen.

→

<-- continued from above

The Tengu explained: In the "dinosaur" experiment it was an issue of not being able to fully connect, rather than an issue of instability or failure to survive. Like food in a nonstick pan, the souls touched them, even leaving a sort of residue, but they did not stick.

The Tengu actually only have a hint of a soul. But, a hint of an eternal everything is quite a bit more than any demon or devil can ever hope to achieve. As a result, they cannot do well against a "true" human, child of God.

Oni does not only describe devils and demons, but rather "metaphysical" beings, in a universal sense.

Net: Oni = Metaphysical Being (universal term)
Tengu = failed "dino" experiment meta-beings (like ghosts, etc.)

Whatever comes in the next 48 hours, the witches will not fare well.

(Symbol with explanation)

←

The Tengu explained: In the "dinosaur" experiment it was an issue of not being able to fully connect, rather than an issue of instability or failure to survive. Like food in a non stick pan, the souls touched them, even leaving a sort of residue, but they did not stick.

The Tengu actually only have a hint of a soul. But, a hint of an eternal everything is quite a bit more than any demon or devil can ever hope to achieve. As a result, they cannot do well against a "true" human, child of God.

Oni does not only describe devils and demons, but rather "metaphysical" beings, in a universal sense.

Net: Oni = Metaphysical Being (universal term)
Tengu = failed "dino" experiment meta-beings (like ghosts, etc.)

Whatever comes in the next 48 hours, the witches will not fair well.

⊙ ← eye
刀 ← claws (4 swords)

(Symbol)

Never forget the formula! It is Everything!

(Symbol)

Never forget who you are! There can only be one!

(Symbol)

Never forget what you are! Life depends upon it!

(Symbol)

Never forget how you got here! Ever!

(Symbol)

Never forget what you have become! It was given!

Not him; The other one …

When the sun sets, it can never be undone! Accept it!

Who is Arthur Conan Stephenson?

(Symbol)

H+D∞
Never forget the formula! It is Everything!

Never forget who you are! There can be only one!

Never forget what you are! Life depend upon it!

Never forget how you get here! Ever!

Never forget what you have become! It was given!

Not him; The other one...
When the sun sets, it can never be undone! Accept it!

Who is Arthur Conan Stephenson?

What comes next has been written about …

… it is not what was written.

What begins, may not end.

What ends, may never have begun.

Forever, Eternity and Everything are not the same thing.

Consider them as dimensions …

… a three-dimensional Eternal Everything Forever is actually possible … now!

Life is Eternal
Substance is Everything
Time is Forever

The absence of any, or one, of these is less. And, when the fight begins, less is the equivalent of nothing.

Infinity and Nothing are not equals!

(Symbol)

If the Bastard is ever awakened …

… the Bastard can/will destroy us all.

What comes next has been written about...
... it is not what was written.

What begins, may not end.
What ends, may never have begun.
Forever, Eternity and Everything are not the same thing.
Consider them as dimensions...
... a three dimensional Eternal Everything Forever
is actually possible ... now!

        Life is Eternal
      Substance is Everything
        Time is Forever

The absence of any, or one, of these is less. And, when the fight begins, less is the equivalent of nothing.

Infinity and Nothing are not equals!

△

If the Bastard is ever awakened...
... The Bastard can/will destroy us all.

Magic and reality are the same.

Magic is any aspect of reality that we cannot identify or understand. To explain what we do not understand, we call it magic, or something like it.

That magic is reality does not indicate that any being within reality can or will be capable of perceiving, and eventually understanding, any and all magic.

Barriers exist. Just as length, width, height, and time are independent states of reality, that can and do exist both in concert and independently of one another, so too do many (but not all) aspects, or if you prefer, dimensions of reality have the capability of coexisting with and without the others.

Ultimately, there are few true limits to what some may perceive, experience or interact with, within reality. Still, limits do exist for some, more than they do for others. There are aspects of reality that some simply cannot ever detect, let alone perceive or understand.
Still others, are incapable of failing to detect, perceive and interact with many, or all, aspects of reality. Call them crazy or call them gods, in truth few gods can ...

continued ->

Magic and reality are the same. Magic is any aspect of reality that we cannot identify or understand. To explain what we do not understand, we call it magic, or something like it.

That magic is reality does not indicate that any being within reality can or will be capable of perceiving, and eventually understanding, any and all magic.

Barriers exist. Just as length, width, height and time are independent states of reality, that can and do exist both in concert and independently of one another, so too do many (but not all) aspects, or if you prefer dimensions of reality have the capability of coexisting with and without the others.

Ultimately, there are few true limits to what some may perceive, experience or interact with, within reality. Still, limits do exist for some, more than they do for others. There are aspects of reality that some simply cannot ever detect, let alone perceive or understand. Still others, are incapable of failing to detect, perceive and interact with many, or all, aspects of reality. Call them crazy or call them gods, in truth few gods can ...

⟶

<-- continued from above

… perceive and understand as much as they think, and wish that they could.

Reality is your own. That others may perceive differing realities from your own, does not indicate that your reality is flawed or incomplete. Similarly, the inverse is also true.

Reality is everything. Anything outside of reality, simply, does not exist. But, of course, that is not the end of it. It is enough, for this reality, for now.

Heaven and Earth (physical existence) are reality. So too, the worlds beyond the veil are reality. The non-realms, such as Chaos, are also reality.

If the all-seeing eye can see it, then it is reality. If there is nothing to see, then it is still reality. God is not only the god of the earth or the physical, or even the metaphysical. God, the one true God, is over everything that is real, everything that is unreal, even everything that does not exist, at all. Everything!

continued ->

←

... perceive and understand as much as they thing, and wish, that they could.

Reality is your own. That others may perceive differing realities from your own, does not indicate that your reality is flawed or incomplete. Similarly, the inverse is also true.

Reality is everything. Anything outside of reality, simply, does not exist. But, of course, that is not the end of it. It is enough, for this reality, for now.

Heaven and Earth (physical existance) are reality. So too, the worlds beyond the veil are reality. The non-realms, such as Chaos, are also reality.

If the all seeing eye can see it, then it is reality. If there is nothing to see, then it is still reality. God is not the only the god of the earth or the physical, or even the meta-physical. God, the one true God, is over everything that is real, everything that is unreal, even everything that does not exist, at all. Everything!

→

<-- continued from above

Outside of what is, there is an infinite that is not. There are no limits. No upper limit. No lower limit. No end and no beginning.

One cannot ever go back to before reality, nor go forward to beyond its end. Reality is all. It is everything that has ever existed, that will ever exist, and also all that does not exist.

As with my bio-dad's patent for "Silence," the reality of that which does not exist, at al, is in fact greater than the reality of what is. Not better, just greater.

To some, this is the great quest, the search for truth and knowledge. For others, this is nothing at all ... they don't even perceive that there is a question.

There can be no end, nor such a thing as too far. It can seem, very much, like there is or there are. But, it is not possible. The real limits are about losing sight of truth and what is right, not how far or how long one journeys.

Do that which is right, always!

←

Outside of what is, there is an infinite that is not. There are no limits. No upper limit. No lower limit. No end and no beginning.

One can not ever go back to before reality, nor go forward to beyond its end. Reality is all. It is everything that has ever existed, that will ever exist, and also all that does not exist.

As with my bio-dad's patent for "Silence", the reality of that which does not exist, at all, is, in fact, greater than the reality of what is. Not better, just greater.

To some, this is the great quest, the search for truth and knowledge. For others, this is nothing at all... they don't even perceive that there is a question.

There can be no end, nor such a thing as too far. It can seem, very much, like there is or there are. But, it is not possible. The real limits are about losing sight of truth and what is right, not how far or how long one journey's.

Do that which is right, always!

12 June 2017, 3:30 am (Pacific)

"Day 7"

— — — — — — — — — — — — — — — —

15 June 2017, 2 am (Pacific)

They tried to take the Phoenix …
I found it on the floor.
I showed them what I am, and spoke;
"Do you fear the darkness? Then, get ready.
I am here."
Midgard took from them, their most cherished prize.
I feed it to the Phoenix. Ooftah!
Then it was said; "The time has come, you are
Unforgiven. It is time to earn your place."
The age of the anti-Christ has begun. I am sad!
I sent three Kings to announce my presence.
I am angry. I am sad. I am disappointed.

From this moment, the age of divine possessors will not see a 100th year.

(Symbol)

12 June 2017, 3:30am (pacific)

"Day 7"

- - - - - - - - - - - - - - - -

15 June 2017, 2am (Pacific)

They tried to take the Phoenix...
I found it on the floor.
I showed them what I am, and spoke;
"Do you fear the darkness? Then, get ready.
I am here."
Midgard took from them, their most cherished prize.
I feed it to the Phoenix. Ooftah!
Then it was said; "The time has come, you are
unforgiven. It is time to earn your place."
The age of the anti-christ has begun. I am sad!
I sent three kings to announce my presence.
I am angry. I am sad. I am disapointed.

From this moment, the age of divine possesers
will not see a 100th year!

Cthulhu / Cthulha / Cthulhin

Trinary beings: Male, Female, Auxiliary

Without the Cthulhin (A), a pair of Cthulhu (M) and Cthulha (F) cannot reproduce, at all.

One (either) generally carries the Cthulhin within them in a symbiotic relationship – much like humans carry the gut bacteria needed to digest food to survive, in protected environments, within but still outside the body.

If Cthulhu and Cthulha are chaotic destructive beings, then Cthulhin are a stabilizing influence that facilitates connection and makes reproduction possible.

Cthulhu: Male, short tentacles
Cthulha: Female, long tentacles
Cthulhin: Auxiliary, round circular and could be mistaken of/for a tentacle "sucker," until it unrolls and "bites" both creatures, holding the connection between them and enabling reproductive transference.

continued ->

Cthulhu / Cthulha / Cthulhin

Trinary beings: Male, Female, Auxillary

Without the Cthulhin (A) a pair of Cthulhu (m) and Cthulha (f) cannot reproduce, at all.

One (either) generally carries the Cthulhin within them in a symbiotic relationship — much like humans carry the gut bacteria needed to digest food, to survive, in protected environments, within but still outside the body.

If Cthulhu and Cthulha are chaotic destructive beings, then Cthulhin are a stabilizing influence that facilitates connection and makes reproduction possible.

Cthulhu: Male, short tentacles
Cthulha: Female, long tentacles
Cthulhin: Auxillary, round circular and could be mistaken of/for a tentacle "sucker", until unrolls and "bites" both creatures, holding the connection between them and enabling reproductive transferance.

→

<-- continued from above

Note: if two Cthulhin carriers encounter each other, they will not reproduce. Nor will either give up the Cthulhin that they carry in order to enable reproduction.

The Nameless One ...

Like air is to humans, so too is fear to chaos. Ti's sister is the storm, the tempest, she sees only the past and orders her world and her way based upon it. Dwelling, to the point of stagnation, on past events, and ancestors, is how she controls and contains people. Her influence was greater than that of Caine. She will, through Zyis, exist within the minds of many. But the immeasurable power behind the nameless images is now lost, forever.

If the creeping chaos is reigned in, so too is the weeping silence forever trapped. And, the Dragon forever King.

Creation happened before the light.

(Symbol) (Symbol)
(Symbol) (Symbol) (Symbol)

←

Note: If two Cthulhin carriers encounter each other, they will not reproduce. Nor will either give up the Cthulhin that they carry in order to enable reproduction.

— — — — — — — — —

The Nameless One...

Like air is to humans, so too is fear to chaos. Ti's sister is the storm, the tempest, she sees only the past and orders her world and her way based upon it. Dwelling, to the point of stagnation, on past events, and ancestors, is how she controls and contains people. Her influence was greater than that of Caine. She will, through Zyis, exist within the minds of many. But, the immeasurable power behind the nameless images is now lost, forever.
If the creeping chaos is reigned in, so too is the weeping silence forever trapped. And, the Dragon forever King.
Creation happened before the light.

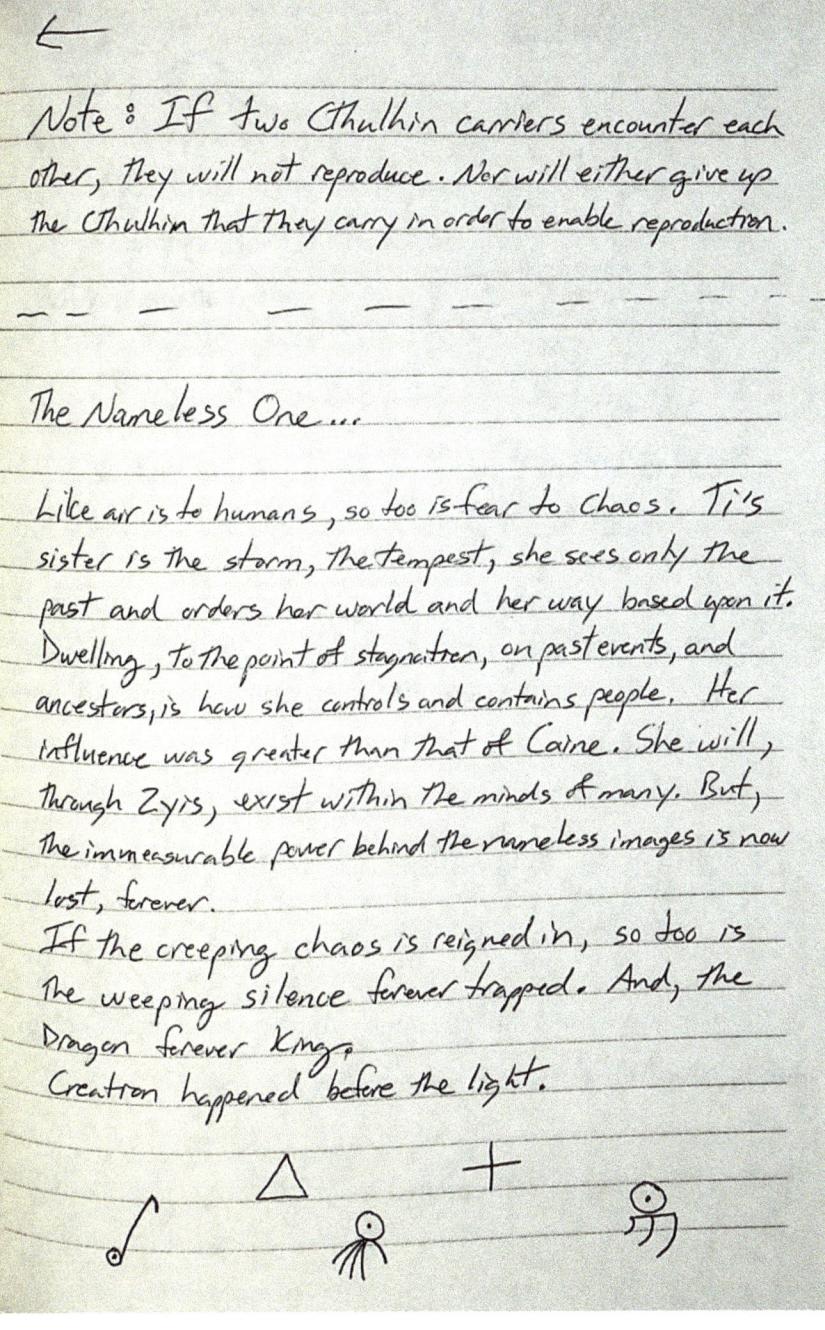

(Symbol) (Symbol)		(Symbol) (Symbol)
Vampire	or	Anpyr
Nyalah		(Personless)
(Queen of Vamps. =		(anti-Light Mites)
Ate her king 😊)		
Take a bite		Infest/infect
And move on.		Drain slowly – forever

— — — — — — — — — — — — — — — —

When God instructs you not to ever write something down, and you do so anyway …

In that moment, you, through your own choice, cease being a prophet of God.

In that moment, you, through your own choice, become a profiteer.

Those who follow a profiteer are rarely following God.

(Symbol)

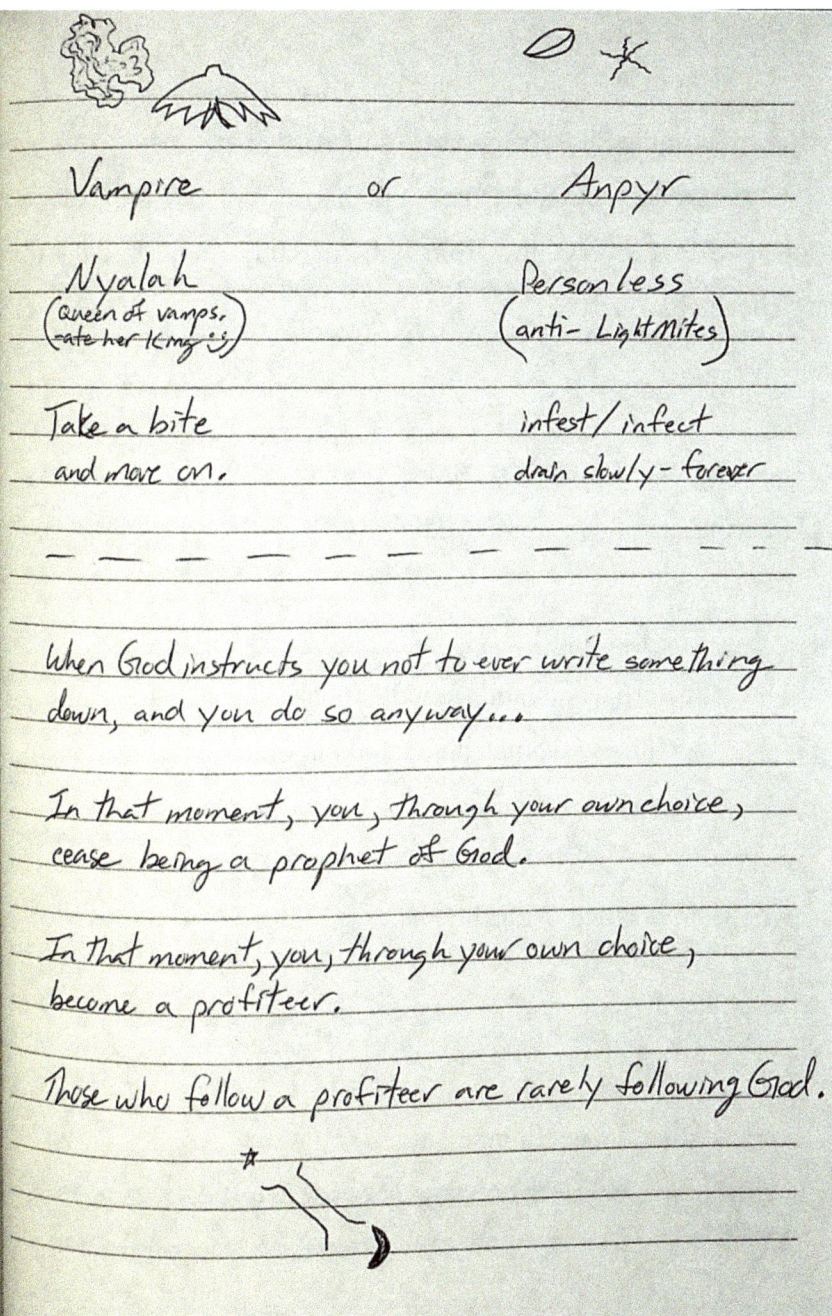

Vampire	or	Anpyr
Nyalah (Queen of vamps, ate her king)		Personless (anti-LightMites)
Take a bite and move on.		infest/infect drain slowly - forever

---

When God instructs you not to ever write something down, and you do so anyway...

In that moment, you, through your own choice, cease being a prophet of God.

In that moment, you, through your own choice, become a profiteer.

Those who follow a profiteer are rarely following God.

They were the "Chosen." Their order had no name.

It started in the First Kingdom, Ada's Kingdom.

They were allied with Caine and his group, but they always planned to take everything from him. In 2007, they thought that their chance had arrived.

Oops!

The Ring, like Caine, is no more.

The Ring, itself, was destroyed!

> The BC ring
> A European woman and her chair
> A Chinese woman and her chair
> A Devil and his ring

Two: Men, Women, Rings, Seats

(Symbol)

There is always something inside!

The Ribbon is no more, too!   No Ring!

They were the "Chosen". Their order had no name.
It started in the first Kingdom, Ada's Kingdom.
They were allied with Caine and his group, but
they allways planned to take everything from him.
In 2007, they thought that their chance had arrived.
Oops!

The Ring, like Caine, is no more.
The Ring, itself, was destroyed!

    The BC ring
      A European Woman and her chair
      A Chinese Woman and her chair
      A Devil and his ring

Two: Men, Women, Rings, Seats

There is always something inside!   No Rings!
The Ribbon is no more, too!

What is Nirvana ...

As the physical beings in multi-cellular beings and each cell has, at its core, the spark of life ...

As a physical starts as a single cell, containing the spark of life ...

As a divine being falls into the single cell of the physical being, like a golden rain falling from every direction, as if a sphere of light particles collapsing in on a singularity of physical life energy ...

As the divine being enters the single living cell, bonding to the spark of life that exists within it, the divine energy pours into the spark as if rain filling a bottomless spherical cup.

When complete, the single living cell begins to replicate. But, instead of a cluster of billions of cells that simply coexist and are related to one another, each connected only to those immediately adjacent, the divine energy connects each individual spark of life, not just to those adjacent, but to each and every spark within the collective being. Every single cell is connected to every other within the life form, by connecting each spark ...

continued ->

What is Nirvana...

As the physical being in multi-cellular beings and each cell has, at its core, the spark of life...

As a physical starts as a single cell, containing the spark of life...

As a divine being falls in to the single cell of the physical being, like a golden rain falling from every direction, as if a sphere of light particles collapsing in on a singularity of physical life energy...

As the divine being enters the single living cell, bonding to the spark of life that exists within it, the divine energy pours into the spark as if rain filling a bottomless spherical cup.

When complete, the single living cell begins to replicate. But, instead of a cluster of billions of cells that simply coexist and are related to one another, each connected only to those immediately adjacent, the divine energy connects each individual spark of life, not just to those adjacent, to each and every spark within the collective being. Every single cell is connected to every other within the life form, by connecting each spark...
→

<-- continued from above

... of life to every other spark, by the presence of the golden divine energy that flows between the sparks like strings of intertwined, interwoven, golden fire ... flowing like fire spreads, or water flows, not like lightning or electricity.

This flow, or transmission, has no speed ... like gravity and Sapphiric energy, it simply is ... any perception of actual "flow" is purely perception!

Achieving a state of being in which one may perceive this aspect of themselves, the divine fire / energy / light flow or rain that creates the impossible presence or network within a life form ....

This is the thing that we call Nirvana!

What's better: finding one's true mate / partner / other-half that allows the impossible 1 to become >2. Nirvana is life, it is not the meaning of life.

Experiencing Nirvana in or during life is not the meaning or goal of life. It is the ultimate ...

continued ->

←

... of life to every other spark, by the presence of the golden divine energy that flows between the sparks like strings of intertwined, interwoven, golden fire... flowing like fire spreads, or water flows, not like lightning or electricity.

This flow, or transmission, has no speed... like gravity and Sapphiric energy it simply is... any perception of actual "flow" is purely perception!

Achieving a state of being in which one may perceive this aspect of themselves, the divine fire/energy/light flow or rain that creates the impossible presence or network within a life form...

This is the thing that we call Nirvana!

What's better: finding one's true mate/partner/other half that allows the impossible 1 to become ≥ 2. Nirvana is life, it is not the meaning of life.

Experiencing Nirvana in or during life is not the meaning or goal of life. It is the ultimate ... →

<-- continued from above

… realization of what we, divine beings, actually are and how much more we are than these simple beings and lives.

In a discussion of life vs. death, the true nature of Nirvana is simply, for us, going home.

We did not come here to figure out how to get home. Rather, we are all going home when we die here.

"While we live we must experience life, limitation, emotion; we must dwell, with intent, within this physical form. Intent is everything." ST (Symbol)

We do not live to escape; we confined ourselves so that we may live. Because of what we experience here, in physical life, when we return home to our natural state, Nirvana, we will then, thanks to our limiting experiences, appreciate and better understand who and what we truly are and how we may be and live better in/as Nirvana.

The, or an, End

←

... realization of what we, divine beings, actually are and how much more we are than these simple beings and lives.

In a discussion of life vs death, the true nature of Nirvana is simply, for us, going home.

We did not come here to figure out how to get home. Rather, we are all going home when we die here.

"While we live we must experience life, limitation, emotion; we must dwell, with intent, within this physical form. Intent is everything." $△

We do not live to escape; we confined ourselves so that we may live. Because of what we experience here, in physical life, when we return home to our natural state, Nirvana, we will then, thanks to our limiting experiences, appreciate and better understand who and what we truly are and how we may be and live better in/as Nirvana.

      The, or an, End

For some, they are not horns:

In the time after we develop the Synthetic Soul Device, there are medical manipulations to our evolution, not inventing new traits but rather, enhancing and expanding traits with perceived value, such as mind reading and enhanced powers of perception.

This first step results in ridges that begin just above the eyebrows and continue under the skin along the skull at the same height as the eardrum. The arc can resemble horns.

As this trend continues, eventually leading to an expansion of the forward and upper portions of the skull, the abilities continue to grow as well.

Ultimately, this pursuit of enhanced sensory perception leads to telepathy and enormous cranial capacity (IE: The Greys and their like).

The earliest examples of this manipulation were most visible as mentalists, intelligence operatives, and so on. Natural occurrence of this trait was first recognized in those who were metaphysically hypersensitive.

For some, they are not horns:

In the time after we develop the Synthetic Soul Device there are medical manipulations to our evolution, not inventing new traits but rather, enhancing and expanding traits with perceived value, such as mind reading and enhanced powers of perception.

This first step results in ridges that begin just above the eyebrows and continue under the skin along the skull, terminating at back of the skull at the same height as the eardrum. The arc can resemble horns.

As this trend continues, eventually leading to an expansion of the forward and upper portions of the skull, the abilities continue to grow as well.

Ultimately, this pursuit of enhanced sensory ~~theory~~ perception leads to telepathy and enormous cranial capacity (IE: the Greys and their like).

The earliest examples of this manipulation were most visible as mentalists, intelligence operatives, and so on. Natural occurance of this trait was first recognized in those who were metaphysically hypersensitive.

07 Sept. 2018

To every warrior comes a day, when they discover that they are not The One, but rather that they are One of. That moment when others are ready, to know the unknown, to see what truths are hidden in the secrets.

One day, it happens to us all … my day was yesterday.

In a moment, the secrets that I keep, the hidden I protect, and the unknown that I know will no longer be mine; they will be ours … again.

Do that which is right, in all ways.

-STX

7 Sept. 2018

To every warrior comes a day, when they discover that they are not The One, but rather that they are One of. That moment when others are ready, to know the unknown, to see what truths are hidden in the secrets.

One day, it happens to us all... my day was yesterday.

In a moment, the secrets that I keep, the hidden I protect, and the unknown that I know will no longer be mine, they will be ours... again.

Do that which is right, in all ways.

"This new order of Knights is one that is unknown by the ages. They fight two wars, one against adversaries of flesh, and another against a spiritual army of wickedness in the heavens."

– St. Bernard

Our Father, who art in heaven
Hallowed be thy name
Thy Kingdom come, Thy Will be done
On earth as it is in heaven
Give us, this day, our daily bread
Do not let us enter into temptation
Deliver us from evil
For Thine is the Kingdom, the Power, and the Glory
Amen

- Our Lord's Prayer

The Templars are His hands
The Dragons are His eyes
The Lions are His voice
Together, they are not Him
Through them, He may be seen

-ST

This new order of knights is one that is
unknown by the ages. They fight two wars,
one against adversaries of flesh, and another
against a spiritual army of wickedness in the
heavens.   — St. Bernard

Our father, who art in heaven
Hollowed be thy name
Thy kingdom come, Thy will be done
On earth as it is in heaven
Give us, this day, our daily bread
Do not let us enter into temptation
Deliver us from evil
For thine is the kingdom, the power, and the glory
Amen
            — Our Lords Prayer

The Templars are his hands
The Dragons are his eyes
The Lions are his voice
Together, they are not him
Through them, he may be seen

Color Plates

Plate 12

Plate 13

Plate 14

Plate 15

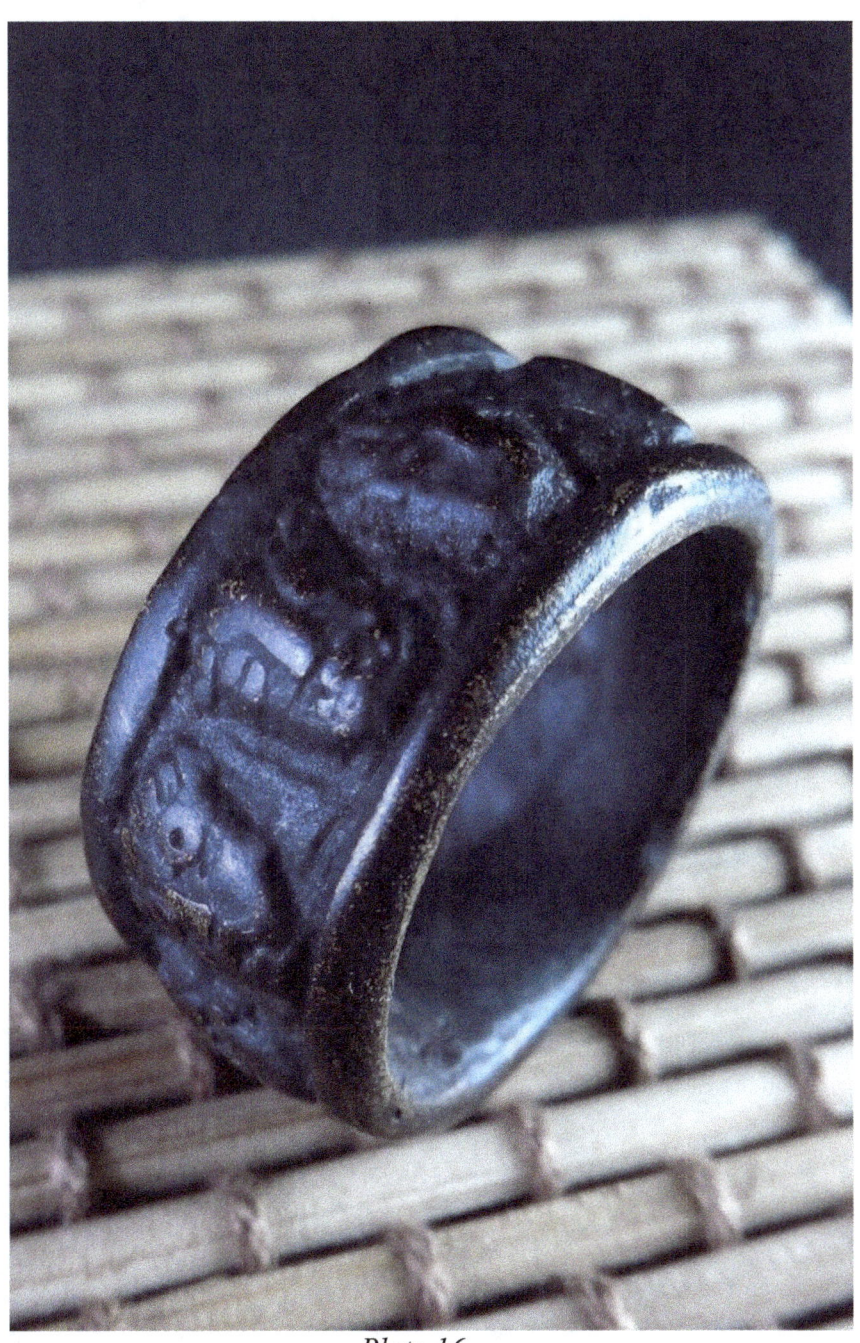

Plate 16

Plate 17

Plate 18

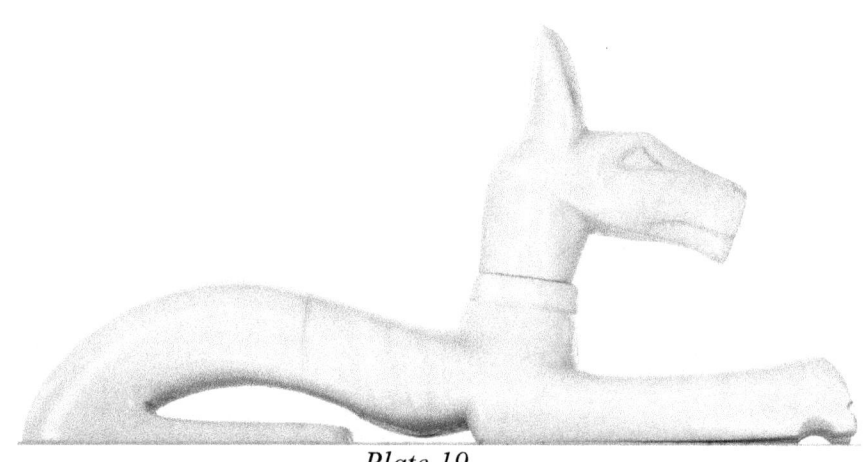

Plate 19

Plate 20

Only our daughter saw, what we all had missed, that the existence of Time, at all, would require the presence of Death, forever.

She chose you, because she saw that you were the one thing that we could not ever create …
… so, she married it.

-Ti

Afterword …   "Destroy what you must."

Long live Death!

The secret of the Necronomicon, the lesson of the ways of old Japan, is not to come to understand and accept all people and the horrible things that they do; rather it is to grasp the danger that the power of creation has bestowed upon us and how it will be used, by some, to corrupt and destroy our home in the same way we have disrupted and destroyed this creation.

The lesson is to come to understand and accept …

continued ->

Only our daughter saw, what we all had missed, that the existence of Time, at all, would require the presence of Death, forever.

She chose you, because she saw that you were the one thing that we could not ever create ...

... so, she married it.
— Ti

Afterword...   "Destroy what you must."

Long live Death!

The secret of the Necronomicon, the lesson of of the ways of old Japan, is not to come to understand and accept all people and the horrible things that they do; rather it is to grasp the danger that the power of creation has bestowed upon us and how it will be used, by some, to corrupt and destroy our home in the same way we have disrupted and destroyed this creation.

The lesson is to come to understand and accept ...
⟶

<-- continued from above

... that there are horrors inside some of us that cannot be allowed to come home, or that must be destroyed if they do ... even if they already are.

We have always needed Death to dwell among us, and now, through creation, it will be able to reach us all. Through Death, those who would destroy everything will, by their own designs, be destroyed.

Death is our salvation. Death shall destroy our way back to peace. Death shall prevent our ultimate path toward corruption and total destruction.

-Ti

... that there are horrors inside some of us that cannot be allowed to come home, or that must be destroyed if they do... even if they already are.

We have always needed Death to dwell among us, and now, through creation, it will be able to reach us all. Through Death, those who would destroy everything will, by their own designs, be destroyed.

Death is our salvation. Death shall destroy our way back to peace. Death shall prevent our ultimate path toward corruption and total destruction.

—T;

Creation of Time

Spiral (Symbol)

Travel in a spiral creates variable time as the passage of time varies depending upon where in the spiral one is.

- In an outer spiral arm time passes more quickly than it does nearer the center of the spiral, Therefore, Spiral Variable Time is relative to one's position or perspective.

Linear (Symbol)

Travel in an absolutely straight line (very hard to do in a spiral universe) creates linear time that is constant in its passage. Regardless of where one exists within the line (string/thread) time passes at the same rate and is therefore, not dependent upon position or perspective.

Parent

Ours is a spiral universe which exists within other spiral universes which exist within linear universes which exist within a single linear parent universe.

continued ->

Creation of Time

Spiral

Travel in a spiral creates variable time as the passage of time varies depending upon where in the spiral one is.
- In an outer spiral arm time passes more quickly than it does nearer the center of the spiral. Therefore, Spiral Variable Time is relative to ones postition or perspective.

Linear

Travel in an absolutely straight line (very hard to do in a spiral universe) creates linear time that is constant in its passage. Regardless of where one exists within the line (string/thread) time passes at the same rate and is, therefore, not dependent upon positron or perspective.

Parent

Ours is a spiral universe which exists within other spiral universes which exist within linear universes which exist within a single linear parent universe.

→

<-- continued from above

Though that linear parent universe is one of many (infinite) that exist, side by side, all traveling in a single direction, along with the spiral parent universes within an eternal and infinite sea universe (seaverse).

Don't Forget! This is all multi-dimensional as well.
                                                    -ST

— — — — — — — — — — — — — — — — —

There are Finite and Infinite at the same time, coexisting, but their relationship is not what we suspect.

"Do not fall victim to mathematics" …
"Like magic, it is only an attempt to make sense of something that is beyond human comprehension."

"The Sea is eternal, there is nothing beyond it."

"Within the Sea there are an infinite number of "strings."
"Within each "string" there are an infinite number of worlds or universes … infinite within infinite … all within infinite, which is, itself, finite."

- Apsu Adam A and Ti Eve An Mat

Through that linear parent universe is one of many (infinite) that exist, side by side, all traveling in a single direction, along with the spiral parent universes within an eternal and infinite sea universe (seaverse).

Don't Forget! This is all multi-dimensional as well.

There are Finite and Infinite at the same time, coexisting, but their relationship is not what we suspect.

"Do not fall victim to mathematics..." like magic, it is only an attempt to make sense of something that is beyond human comprehension.

"The Sea is eternal, there is nothing beyond it."

Within the Sea there are an infinite number of "strings". Within each "string" there are an infinite number of worlds or universes... infinite within infinite... all within infinite, which is, itself, finite.
— Apsu Adam A and Ti Eve An Mat

"A man alone is but a man; A man and a woman together are a creator."

— — — — — — — — — — — — — — — —

Primordial Sea – black and seemingly empty, but it isn't

(Symbol)

continued ->

"A man alone is but a man; A man and a woman together are a creator."

― ― ― ― ― ― ― ― ― ―

Primordial Sea — black and seemingly empty, but it isn't.

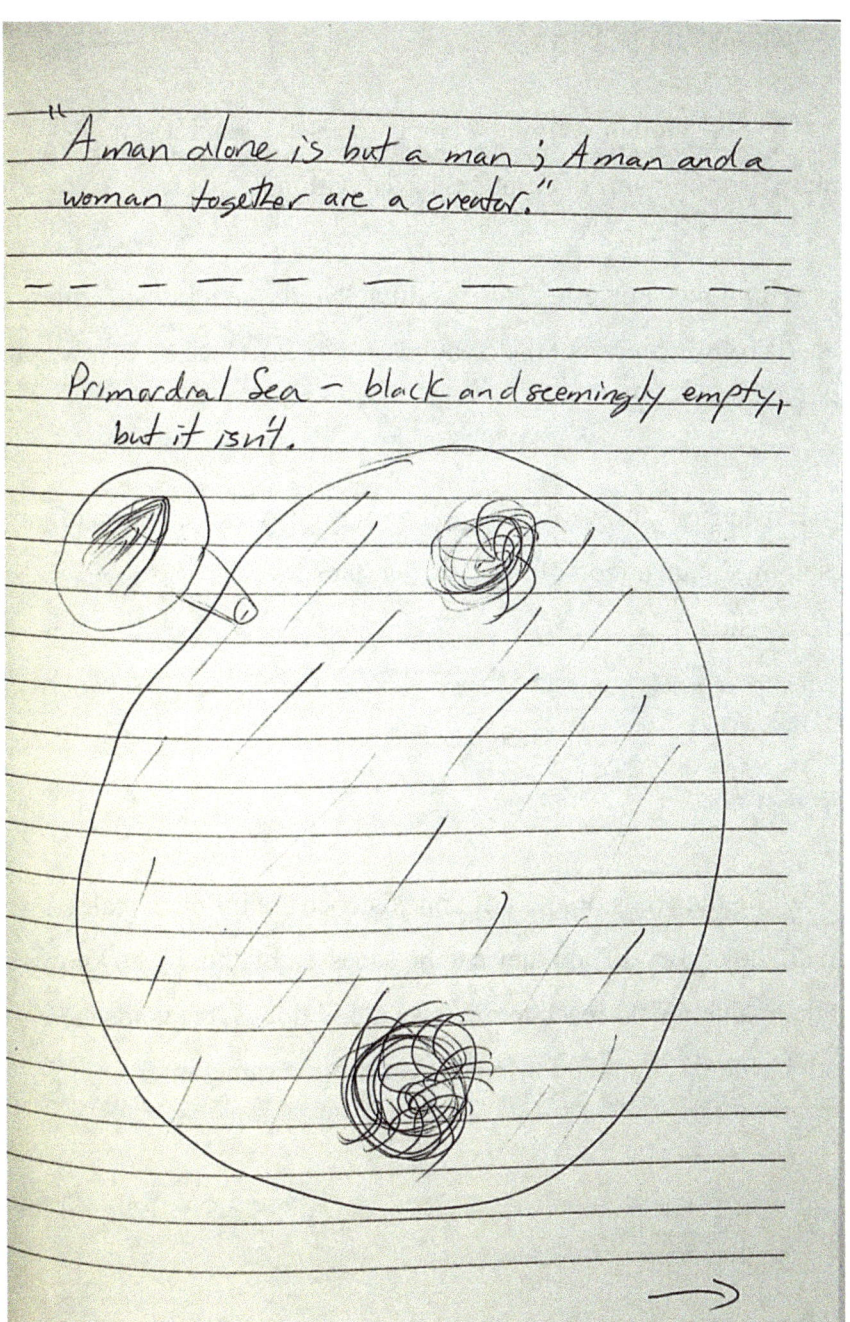

→

<-- continued from above

The Sea, though seemingly empty, does exist and it is not empty. Nor do voids of emptiness exist within it.

Within the "universes" the resulting "voids" are, in fact, empty and, therefore, represent the creation of non-existence by that which does exist.

Existence is forever, while nonexistence is/was a creation of, or result of, the invention of Time by that/those which/who exist/existed.

(Symbol)

While the voids or areas of nonexistence are infinitesimally small, they do exist, and they can be accessed by those who know of them and how to reach them. As with all things, the voids are both infinitely small and infinitely large at the same time.

Don't get trapped!

←

The Sea, though seemingly empty, does exist and it is not empty. Nor do voids of emptiness exist within it.

Within the "universes" the resulting "voids" are, in fact, empty and, therefore, represent the creation of non-existance by that which does exist.

Existance is forever, while non existance is/was a creation of, or result of, the invention of Time by that/those which/who exist/existed.

→ creation of voids or nonexistance

While the voids or areas of none existance are infinitesimally small, they do exist and they can be accessed by those who know of them and how to reach them. As with all things, the voids are both infinitely small and infinitely large at the same time.

Don't get trapped!

This War

Or, Persephone's Return From Hades

In this war, there are no victims, only volunteers.
While most fight for life, we fight for right.
Will I die for what is right … I already have.
I will again, if it is right, as many times as I must.
Why do we fight … to seek the light beyond nothing.
This war, we have already won … but, they fight on.
When it ends, we will be more and they will not be
When it ends, there will be no more, this war.

01-09-2018   -ST

This War

Or, Persephone's Return From Hades

In this war, there are no victims,
  only volunteers.
While most fight for life, we fight for
  right.
Will I die for what is right... I already
  have.
I will again, if it is right, as many times
  as I must.
Why do we fight... to seek the light beyond
  nothing.
This war, we have already won... but, they
  fight on.
When it ends, we will be more and they
  will not be.
When it ends, there will be no more, this
  war.

1-9-2018

Our Journey

When crazy becomes normalcy

When popularity becomes trust

When we stop seeking the light

When we accept emptiness and darkness as one, the same

In this world, when these things happen, this is when …

When we must prove the light

When we must be the light

When only the light remains, continues on

This is when we will be home, at peace

This is when time stops, forever begins

Home, Forever, in Peace

Our journey, together

01-10-2018 -ṢT

Our Journey

When crazy becomes normalcy
When popularity becomes trust
When we stop seeking the light
When we accept emptiness and darkness
      as one, the same
In this world, when these things happen,
      this is when...
When we must prove the light
When we must be the light
When only the light remains, continues on
This is when we will be home, at peace
This is when time stops, forever begins
Home, Forever, in Peace
Our journey, together

1-10-2018

Kaine's Children

Like the proverbial Dr. Frankenstein, Kaine sought to create life, children, because he could not do so himself. He chose to subject creation to his will. From the depths of the flood waters he struck at God, at what he had created for us.

He used a witch, a Redwood tree, and an ape. The witch carried the egg, the ape planted the seed, the Redwood provided a home, a womb.

Within the roots of the tree, she was held, while the ape dwelt above, protecting the tree and her egg. The ape never let go of that Redwood and the tree never let go of the witch. The three acted as one.

When it was done, the result was two children. There was a boy and a girl. They were the first of their kind. They were an abomination, a distortion of God's created Nature. Unreal, but real!

They were made, manipulated, a warping of natural law to create an earthly physical binary source, tethered to each other, not to the heavens. Unnatural physical / metaphysical earthly life …

The Children of Kaine   -ST

Kaine's Children

Like the proverbial Dr. Frankenstein, Kaine sought to create life, children, because he could not do so himself. He chose to subject creation to his will. From the depths of the flood waters he struck at God, at what he had created for us.

He used a witch, a Redwood tree, and an ape. The witch carried the egg, the ape planted the seed, the Redwood provided a home, a womb.

Within the roots of the tree, she was held, while the ape dwelt above, protecting the tree and her egg. The ape never let go of that Redwood and the tree never let go of the witch. The three acted as one.

When it was done, the result was two children. There was a boy and a girl. They were the first of their kind. They were an abomination, a distortion of God's created Nature. Unreal, but real!

They were made, manipulated, a warping of natural law to create an earthly physical binary source, tethered to each other, not to the heavens. Unnatural physical/metaphisical earthly life...

The Children of Kaine

Time Line of US

Civilization, as a whole, rises and falls. Whether by weather or catastrophe or outside intervention, the whole of human civilization comes and goes.

The frequency is unstable and the amplitude varies, but, like the sun, what rises will fall. And, what falls will rise again. It is below as it is above. It is without as it is within. It is, as are, until it is not.

    1,283,000 ya: Eve (it begins)　　　　　Rise!　An
      800,000 ya: A new civilization period　　Rise!　Nu
      300,000 ya: a new civilization period　　Rise!　Na
      100,000 ya: Proto-Giza civilization begins　Rise!　Ki
       70,000 ya: The Proverbial Flood – start glacial period
       38,000 ya: Giza civilization expands again
   36-34,000 ya: The Builders: Sphinx and Pyramids at Giza
       26,000 ya: Begin Glacial Maximum period
       13,000 ya: End Glacial Maximum period
       10,000 ya: Begin Interglacial period of the Ice Age in which we (US) currently live. Warm enough!

300 years from now, it gets cold fast. (only 5% survive)
By this time, the Ki will be gone from this universe.

Time Line of US

Civilization, as a whole, rises and falls. Whether by weather or catastrophe or outside intervention, the whole of human civilization comes and goes. The frequency is unstable and the amplitude varies, but, like the Sun, what rises will fall. And, what falls will rise again. It is below as it is above. It is without as it is within. It is, as we are, until it is not.

1,283,000 mya : Eve (it begins)   Rise! An
800,000 ya : A new civilization period   Rise! Nu
300,000 ya : A new civilization period   Rise! Na
100,000 ya : Proto Giza civilization begins   Rise! Ki
70,000 ya : The Proverbial Flood - start glacial period
38,000 ya : Giza civilization expands again
36-34,000 ya : The Builders : Sphinx and Pyramids at Giza
26,000 ya : Begin Glacial Maximum period
13,000 ya : End Glacial Maximum period
10,000 ya : Begin Interglacial period of the Ice Age in
           which we (us) currently live. Warm enough!

300 years from now, it gets cold fast. (only 5% survive)
    by this time, the Ki will be gone from this universe

Four God Killers are one, again. Four nails have rejoined The Lance. Four Men are now one. And, Four Directions are now all.

The Dragon King has five claws, but the fifth is actually the result of all four combined. It is unique and different, but without the four, it could not be.

(Symbol) (Symbol) (Symbol) (Symbol)

The created Witchverse is gone; nothing took its place.
The mechanism that created it will never be again. If one were to go looking, they would find emptiness…
… not nirvana, not completion, but absence …
… only absolute absence.   Don't look!

Witches, Warlocks, Devils, and Demons … all of the things that choose to strike fear in good hearts … all of those beings … the ones that chose wrong … all of them are lost. The age of forgiveness has passed; The age of judgement has begun. Judgement's feather touch is light, but it breaks even the strongest backs.

Do that which is right, always!   (Symbol)

Four God Killers are one, again. Four nails have rejoined The Lance. Four Men are now one. And, Four Directions are now all.

The Dragon King has five claws, but the fifth is actually the result of all four combined. It is unique and different, but without the four, it could not be.

8 ∞ 8 ∞

The created Witchverse is gone; nothing took it's place. The mechanism that created it will never be again. If one were to go looking, they would find emptiness...
... not nirvana, not completion, but absence ...
... only absolute absence. Don't look!

Witches, Warlocks, Devils, and Demons ... all of the things that choose to strike fear in good hearts ... all of those beings ... the ones that chose wrong ... all of them are lost. The age of forgiveness has passed; The age of judgement has begun. Judgement's feather touch is light, but it breaks even the strongest backs.

Do That which is right, always!

Endings

Within the light, there is darkness.

Within the darkest, there is light.

Redemption is not ever impossible, unless, for you, it is.

Forgiveness was, once, freely given.

It seems, all things do come to an end.

If you seek the light, it will see you looking.

If you seek only darkness, it is easily found.

What once was lost, may forever be so.

What goes unfound, will not ever have been.

-ST

I once saw a witch eat a baby. I once saw a warlock kill his wife. I once saw a body turned lantern. I once saw sacrifice sold as life.

I have seen more. I have seen worse. I have seen.

I have done what many thought evil. In darkness, I have shown light. I have eaten my enemies, devoured their souls ... I have always done what was right.

I have done more. I have done worse. I have done.

-ST

Endings

Within the light, there is darkness.
Within the darkest, there is light.
Redemption is not ever impossible, unless, for you, it is.
Forgiveness was, once, freely given.
It seems, all things do come to an end.
If you seek the light, it will see you looking.
If you seek only darkness, it is easily found.
What once was lost, may forever be so.
What goes unfound, will not ever have been.

$

‐ ‐ ‐ ‐ ‐ ‐ ‐ ‐

I once saw a witch eat a baby. I once saw a warlock kill his wife. I once saw a body turned lantern. I once saw sacrifice sold as life.

I have seen more. I have seen worse. I have seen.

I have done what many thought evil. In darkness, I have shown light. I have eaten my enemies, devoured their souls... I have always done what was right.

I have done more. I have done worse. I have done. $

Children

We no longer throw children from boats, to see if they learn how to swim.

We no longer leave children in darkness, to see if they kill what comes after them.

These things that we do, to protect them from strife,
They are things that we do, to lengthen their life.

No consideration at all, for a life that is earned.
Just life, nothing more … books and souls are all burned.

-ST

— — — — — — — — — — — — — — — — —

Magicians seek Faustian moments, then write sonnets of how they survived. What we never see, we think cannot be, is what happens behind the other side's eyes.

— — — — — — — — — — — — — — — — —

If an angel asked you for help, would you ask them anything? Now, what if it were a devil, asking for help … would you ask anything?
  What do they ask of you, when you ask for help?!?!

Children

We no longer throw children from boats, to see if they learn how to swim.

We no longer leave children in darkness, to see if they kill what comes after them.

These things that we do, to protect them from strife, they are things that we do, to lengthen their life.

No consideration at all, for a life that is earned. Just life, nothing more ... books and souls are all burned.

Magicians seek Faustian moments, then write sonets of how they survived. What we never see, we think cannot be, is what happens behind the other side's eyes.

If an angel asked you for help, would you ask them anything? Now, what if it were a devil, asking for help ... would you ask them anything? What do they ask of you, when you ask for help?!?!

"You are the only thing standing between reality and truth."

-Ada

I once saw a man, of sorts, whose face was like that of a human, but with sunken features and sharp pointed rough teeth. His torso was like a well-muscled man, as was his right arm. His left arm was a strong feathered wing. His left leg was hooved (two toed) and his right leg was scaled, like that of a bird, with a taloned four clawed bird foot. I sensed a tail, but I could not see one. His eyes were grey. His skin was dark, almost like burnt charcoal, with flecks of grey within it. He had no hair, nor clothes, nor genitals.

I trapped the creature, or man, and held him as he faced another man, whom he had tortured as a boy. As the survivor raised a wooden hammer and pointed it at the creature, asking, "Do you remember me?" – The creature could only look away, in shame. At that moment, judgement came. The creature was lost to the darkness – cast into the pit … never to be seen again.

While, the survivor lives on … forever.

(Symbol)

"You are the only thing standing between reality and truth."
— Ada

I once saw a man, of sorts, whose face was like that of a human, but with sunken features and sharp pointed rough teeth. His torso was like a well muscled man, as was his right arm. His left arm was a strong feathered wing. His left leg was hooved (two toed) and his right leg was scaled, like that of a bird, with a tallored four clawed bird foot. I sensed a tail, but I could not see one. His eyes were grey. His skin was dark, almost like burnt charcoal, with flecks of grey within it. He had no hair, nor clothes, nor genitals. I trapped the creature, or man, and held him as he faced another man, whom he had tortured as a boy. As the survivor raised a wooden hammer and pointed it at the creature; asking, "Do you remember me?" — The creature could only look away, in shame. At that moment, judgement came. The creature was lost to the darkness — cast in to the pit... never to be seen again. While, the survivor lives on ... forever.

Dragons

In 1918 a Chinese professor spotted a Blue Dragon as it slipped into a river.

In 2007 an American Doctor saw a Blue Dragon devour an enormous serpent, or snake, in Russia.

In an undocumented deep water experiment, an American Advanced Technology expert watched a silver/grey Dragon fly through the depths of the Pacific as birds do, in the air.

A woman, with a master's degree, lost control of her car in ice and snow. She felt one side of her car lift off of the ground … and then saw a silver/white Dragon push her car back down to the ground and the car came to a stop. There were no signs of impact.

I do not share these accounts to convince you that dragons are, or were, real. But rather, to point out that educated observers report seeing things, that they saw clearly, and understood what they were seeing, and felt compelled to share. But, eyewitness testimony is not enough for our skeptical modern minds to consider. That is why we fail to see so much of the universe around us.

In 1918 a Chinese Professor spotted a Blue Dragon as it slipped into a river.

In 2007 an American Doctor saw a Blue Dragon devour an enormous serpent, or snake, in Russia.

In an undocumented deep water experiment, an American Advanced Technology expert watched a silver/grey Dragon fly through the depths of the Pacific as birds do, in the air.

A woman, with a Masters Degree, lost control of her car in ~~icy~~ ice and snow. She felt one side of her car lift off of the ground... and then saw a silver/white Dragon push her car back down to the ground and the car came to a stop. There were no signs of impact.

I do not share these accounts to convince you that dragons are, or were, real. But rather, to point out that educated observers report seeing things, that they saw clearly, and understood what they were ~~seeing~~, and felt compelled to share. But, eye witness testimony is not enough for our skeptical modern minds even to consider. That is why we fail to see so much of the universe around us.

Out of the darkness they came

A truth more pure than in any kingdom

They do not fear the light

Nor do they need it to see

Their King is the darkness itself

Still too, their King is one of them

They owe no one

They collect everything

For it is how they show you what they are

It is how they show you that they are

They teach us all

Yet most of us never see them

They are not gods

They are not monsters

What they are is always what we need

They are forever

They are Dragons

-SX

Out of the darkness they came
A truth more pure than in any kingdom
They do not fear the light
Nor do they need it to see
Their King is the darkness itself
Still too, their King is one of them
They owe no one
They collect everything
For it is how they show you what they are
It is how they show you that they are
They touch us all
Yet most of us never see them
They are not gods
They are not monsters
What they are is always what we need
They are forever
They are Dragons

Listen to the Sphinx

In Giza, near the great pyramids and their sphinx, there is an (as of yet) undiscovered chamber.

Called, The Chamber of Light or the Anti-Darkness Chamber; it houses / holds the secrets of Saph, the secrets of Sapphire (Corundum, Ruby, Al_2O_3).

The chamber teaches such secrets as, the volume of physical existence that may be cleaned / cleansed / cleared by a given weight of White Sapphire.

Much of the Knowledge that has been lost, regarding Sapphiric Energy, is recorded in this chamber. An interesting note: each of the pyramid + sphinx complexes around the world have a similar chamber. Each location teaches the secrets of a type of stone or crystal.

Unlike Giza, many of the pyramid + sphinx complexes are of pre-flood construction. As such, the locations are quite challenging to locate and explore.

Sphinx are Keepers of secrets. One day, they will give them back to us.

Listen to the Sphinx

In Giza, near the great pyramids and their Sphinx, there is an (as of yet) undiscovered chamber. Called, The Chamber of Light or The Anti-Darkness Chamber; it houses/holds the secrets of Saph, the secrets of Sapphire (Corundum, Ruby, Al_2O_3).

The chamber teaches such secrets as, the volume of physical existance that may be cleaned/cleansed/cleared by a given weight of White Sapphire.

Much of the Knowledge that has been lost, regarding Sapphiric Energy, is recorded in this chamber. An interesting note: each of the pyramid + sphinx complexes around the world have a similar chamber. Each location teaches the secrets of a type of stone or crystal.

Unlike Giza, many of the pyramid + sphinx complexes are of pre-flood construction. As such, the locations are quite challenging to locate and explore.

Sphinx are Keepers of secrets. One day, they will give them back to us.

...**End**

Appendix: A Templar's Thoughts

Today is one of those days. It's the sort of day that reminds me of something that a wise person once said, to me: "Once you understand the truth of how things actually are, in this world... once you see what things truly are and grasp how they can be so... then you will understand the terrors of this world, how much worse it actually is... and, why it is that you have absolutely nothing to fear".

So, don't panic. Today is just one of those days, for many. Stay strong, be safe, and remember who we are.

The most cleverly packaged messages and marketing will invariably present the intended victim with a question of This OR That, because once the binary conflict mechanism, within the mind, is engaged it becomes almost impossible for the intended victim to ask the question of whether or not either, This OR That, are both true, or if both are false.

This is true in sales, relationships, media, politics, and even in the hard sciences and the social sciences. This is not to suggest that all binary decisions are traps or manipulation, but rather it is a warning to be cautious, lest you be tricked into making a decision regarding A vs B, when the true answer, the safe answer, is actually C.

Dignity: It is not something that one losses. Dignity is taken from us, by others. It is taken from others, by us.
The value of dignity cannot be over stated. Remember what it is worth, before you take it from someone.

One day, a man was running, panicked, through a thick forest when, suddenly, he came upon an old brick house. He knocked upon the door, nervously waiting, hoping that someone would answer.
When the door opened, a small man, supported by a cane, welcomed him with a friendly smile.
How may I help you; the small man asked.
The panicked man replied; Please help me, I am being chased through these woods, by something evil and dark, something unlike anything else I have ever seen.
The small man simply smiled and welcomed the stranger inside, asking only; Which one?

I just saw something. I cannot tell you what, nor how I saw it. What I saw was unimaginable...
All I can say is: Pray, to God. Just pray. Or else, one day you will wish that you had done so.
Do that which is right, always.

Where there is freedom, there will be conflict.
Where no freedom exits, there will be conflict.
Where there is disparity, there will be greed.
Where no disparity exists, greed will create disparity.
Neither freedom or a lack thereof, nor disparity or a lack thereof can ever eliminate greed and conflict from our world.
Such ideas are actually ideals. Ideals are rarely actualized. And, Ideals are never actualized by committee.
We may dream of ideals, and we should. But, to live as though you exist in an ideal world is turn a blind eye to the reality of conflict, greed and other destructive forces, it is to turn a blind eye to nature itself.
Aim high! But, live today.

I once saw a man, standing at the edge, atop a tall tower; he was afraid to look down, for fear that someone might reach up and pull him off, taking from him the heights he had achieved.
I once saw a man, standing in the muck, deep in a dark pit; he was afraid to look up, for fear that someone might look down upon him, revealing to him the depths to which he had fallen.
Do not fear those who would reach up to you, they might just need a hand to lift them up.
Do not fear those who would look down upon you, they might be offering a hand, to you.
Always look, for if you do not then the truth may be hidden from you.
Always reach, for if you do not then someone may suffer.
You have nothing to fear, beit in the pit or atop the tower, for there is nothing that can harm the divine... and, you are that.

Let us not pretend that these issues are isolated to the rich and powerful of Hollywood, that is meant as a distraction. These are global infestations, that have penetrated the defenses of every nation, every government, every large city, every large corporation, etc.

My whole life has been the great work of finding, penetrating and weakening such groups and organizations. The light that we have shown upon them has finally revealed them, some of them, and the extent of the danger is so great that they would sacrifice Hollywood, in an attempt to survive.

Today, we celebrate Christopher Columbus. And, we should! He certainly was not the original discoverer of the Americas, but he was responsible for opening a door that few believed existed.

By traveling to the Americas, in such a glorious and public manner, Columbus, and his crew, made believers out of experts and skeptics who, themselves, were certain no such lands existed and taught everyone to believe as they did. (They did not believe because references to the existence of the Americas were cleverly hidden away... in books and on maps... that the experts didn't accept as evidence... sound familiar!?!?)

Without that journey of discovery, we may never have become the United States of America.

Certainly, Columbus was not the first, nor even the tenth; he was, however, the person who made most of the rest of us believe.

Happy Columbus day.

While I appreciate this revelation a great deal, it is important that I remind people of is this simple comparison:
If we, as humans (a singular human) can be represented as the number 8.
Our spirit, or soul, that is projected here would be equivalently represented as the number 1677740000000000.
And, that is just the tiny measurable bit of our true selves that we project here, to this physical creation.
It's all good, but this is some perspective... to keep it real.

We who dwelt on high, were the chosen.
Those who dwelt below, were the snakes of the earth.
As the year ends, we are no longer divided.
As the new year begins, we all belong to God.
- thus endeth the year 5777... thus begineth the year 5778 -
Amen

The vast technology and information gaps have always existed between the "real" world and the secret world. What has changed is that we have now created yet another world between them, the world of governance, industry and military (or, as I like to call it: the MiG world).
The real world is dominated by popularism, it includes almost everyone as well as all media.
The MiG world is dominated by insiderism, it is includes most of the government, major industrial powers, the top tier law enforcement, the military.
The secret world is dominated by secretism, it holds secrets as though they are life giving breaths of air; if they are ever released then they are lost.
This is why the people don't know we are at war, and why the governing bodies seem so unaware of the actual secrets.

August 9th
For those who know to what I am referring, as of today there is no Ring, they're done.
Do that which is right, always.

If you want peace, prepare for war.
If you want war, just wait, one's always coming.
If you want to be conquered, then unilaterally disarm.
If you want to be conquered internally, without war, then disarm your populace.

As creation occurred before the light...
If the creeping chaos is reigned in...
So too, is the weeping silence forever trapped...
And, the Dragon forever King.

I don't know why this popped in to my head, but I was suddenly reminded of something that someone said to me once, regarding his time among the Tengu people. He said: "They are a lot more like birds than people are, but then they are a lot more like people than birds are."

This is not meant to be a "lesson", just food for thought. If that doesn't make any sense to you, don't worry about it, remember that I am a crackpot and go on about your business.

Truth is like a Dragon's horde: Many will proclaim it cannot be, most others will believe them. Then, one day, someone will stumble upon one; either they will keep it for themselves, or they will share it; either way, many will proclaim it cannot be...
Take from it what you will. But, share it so that others can know truth.

The voices in your head are like advertisers, news media and politicians: There is truth in what they say, but not all of what they say is true.

Crackpotism:
When Lincoln referenced it, the state of the world was such that most people viewed the very idea of putting an end to slavery as crackpotism.
Not long ago, the same could be said of the concept of same sex marriage.
In Lincoln's time, the very idea of something travelling faster than sound was crackpotism.
Not long ago, the same could be said regarding time travel.
The point is not that every crackpot idea has merit, nor even that every crackpot is sane.
The point is that people change and their understanding of what is and what is not also changes.
To some, the rules are written in stone. To others, stones are just building material that has yet to be reshaped; whatever may be written upon them will change as the stones change.

They say that the truth will set you free...
But, what they do not tell you is: If you accidentally take the wrong fork somewhere along the path to truth, your truth may actually be a prison.
I believe in absolute religious freedom, provided that the practices of all religions do not have an extreme demonstrable negative impact on the other religious people's freedom (IE: my religion requires the killing or enslavement of anyone not in my religion / or my religion allows for the sacrifice or torture of unwilling or unknowing human life)
Beware the leopard. Slay the serpent. Do that which is right, always.

I was having a conversation with an old friend, when I was reminded of something said to me long ago, by someone of great wisdom:
"It is the adversary who is aware that you are coming, yet does not move, that is truly worth facing."
- An Old Man On A Mountain

Secrets and lies are part of governance; beit parents or governments, such thing are a necessary part of protecting the governed.
When secrets and lies become corruption is when they are no longer used to protect the governed, but are instead used to manipulate them and to protect the the governor's from their own mistakes, failures and crimes.

"If your theory is right, there is a good chance we are going to get killed anyway. So we might as well try and find out why."
- A Nun called Sarah

As you study the fields of grass, remember that it is not the grass you seek. But, the grass will show you where to find that which you seek.

Skill and vigilance are not enough, one needs luck as well.

"We must always take sides. Neutrality helps the oppressor, never the victim. Silence encourages the tormentor, never the tormented." -Elie Wiesel
The ability to discern between the oppressor and the oppressed is paramount before we take sides. Silence may not help the tormented, but encouragement frequently helps the tormentor.

Sometimes it's easy to tell the good guy from the bad. Other times it isn't. The question is: How will you determine which is which when your time comes?

Remember, just because it looks like it should not be, does not indicate that it is not. What we call impossible is often simply that which we do not yet believe, or understand.

When one excludes the heart from the decision making process, they are excluding the one part of themselves that can, quite literally, see / sense the future.
When the future is no longer part of the decision making process, much has been lost. This is, in part, because the mind can be fooled.
Educate your mind and always trust your heart.

There can be no rational reason why one would stand against Elohim; rebel against God. I liken those that do to teenagers, rebelling against their parents because the teens are so upset about being wrong all the time.

Eventually, the teens will learn that their parents, like God, were actually trying to help them all along. Perhaps that is one of the meanings of life: To learn to recognize the difference between those who truly stand against us and those who are trying to help and protect us, even from ourselves.

Stop sacrificing your mental, emotional and physical health at the altar of the politics gods.

It's all make believe: It's a puppet show that is only intended to distract and herd us.

Like a herding dog runs around the herd barking and scaring every member into doing exactly what the shepherd wants, so too are politics and media.

Those that wish to control the future of human society send herding dogs, in the form of media scare tactics, to rile us up and push us in the direction desired.

They divide us in order to better control smaller herds.

They distract us with a puppet show, called politics, which is absolutely meaningless and completely outside of our control. That way we will not realize that we are powerless nor recognize the danger, that the so called shepherds are driving us exactly where they want us.

Start learning and thinking for yourself and for your children. Stop regurgitating whatever you are tricked into eating.

Ignore politics, the puppet show.

Follow your own path, not the one you are herded down.

Celebrate and enjoy your life and the lives of those close to you, not the carefully manipulated public relations stories of imaginary lives.

Eat, drink and be merry. While you still can.

The inability to express what you know to be true in a way that convinces others that you are correct, or that they are incorrect, does not necessarily indicate that your message is false.
Case in point: Noah! Every culture in the world remembers "the man in a boat."
Plenty of people had the opportunity to listen and hear the truth. But they were so convinced of their own superiority or the superiority of the people that they wanted to believe that they were completely blind to the truth. Right up until their lungs filled with water.
Decide what you believe and act on it. Not what you want to believe, but what you know, deep down in your soul, is true.
Am I a crackpot? And, whether I am or not, are the things that I have said actually true?

Look to the light. Seek out those who bring illumination to your life. Be a beacon on the hill for others to seek. Breathe peace unto this earth. Create a safe haven from the darkness looming on the horizon. For the Lord God has said Love Everyone.

www.ingramcontent.com/pod-product-compliance
Lightning Source LLC
Chambersburg PA
CBHW051936290426
44110CB00015B/1995